Staffing for Results

A Guide to Working Smarter

DIANE MAYO
JEANNE GOODRICH
FOR THE
**Public Library
Association**

American Library Association
Chicago and London
2002

While extensive effort has gone into ensuring the reliability of information appearing in this book, the publisher makes no warranty, express or implied, on the accuracy or reliability of the information, and does not assume and hereby disclaims any liability to any person for any loss or damage caused by errors or omissions in this publication.

Project manager: Joan A. Grygel

Cover and text design: Dianne M. Rooney

Composition: the dotted i in Stempel Schneidler and Univers using QuarkXpress 4.01 on a Macintosh

Printed on 50-pound white offset, a pH-neutral stock, and bound in 10-point coated cover stock by McNaughton & Gunn

The paper used in this publication meets the minimum requirements of American National Standard for Information Sciences—Permanence of Paper for Printed Library Materials, ANSI Z39.48-1992. ∞

ISBN 0-8389-0826-8

Printed in the United States of America.

06 05 04   5 4 3 2

Contents

Figures   **v**

Acknowledgments   **vii**

Introduction   **ix**

Chapter 1   **Keys to Success**   **1**

Work Is Changing   3

Staff Time—A Limited Resource   4

Decisions Require Data   6

What Is Workload Analysis?   7

Issues to Address   12

Communicating Effectively   13

Forming an Advisory Group   16

Do It Only if You Will Use It   17

Using This Book   20

Chapter 2   **Design Your Project**   **21**

Required Planning   22

Understanding Project Management   28

Defining Your Workload Analysis Project   36

Chapter 3   **Basic Numeric Analysis**   **42**

Using Existing Output Data   43

Establishing Baseline Measurements   45

Developing Data on Effort   46

Establishing the Link between Effort and Output   52

Comparing Baseline Measures   57

Chapter 4   **Basic Process Analysis**   **61**

Choosing to Analyze Process   62

Deciding What You Need to Know   63
Analyzing the Data   66

Chapter 5   **Beyond the Basics**   **77**

Analyzing Numeric Measures   78
Detailed Process Analysis   86

Chapter 6   **Act on What You Learn**   **94**

Communicating the Results   95
Dealing with Change and Resistance   99
Implementation   105
The Cycle of Improvement   108

Instructions and Workforms   **111**

1   Workload Analysis Project Overview   112
2   Estimate of Productive Work Hours Available   117
3   Determining Who Does What   120
4   Standard Terms in Our Library for Tasks and Steps   122

General Instructions for Analysis of Staff Time   126
5   Analysis of Staff Time: Work Unit Estimate of Time Spent on Activities   127
6   Analysis of Staff Time: Individual Estimate of Time Spent on Activities   129

General Instructions for Recording Staff Tasks   131
7   Recording Staff Tasks: Self-Report Log   132
8   Recording Staff Tasks: Direct Observation Log   135

General Instructions for Analysis of a Task   139
9   Analysis of a Task:
     Observation   140
     Self Report   142

10   Time Spent on an Input-Driven Task   145
11   Time Spent on a Demand-Driven Task   148
12   Time Spent on Public Desks   151
13   Workflow Chart   154

Index   **157**

Figures

1	Activity/Task/Step Relationship	8
2	Example of a Set of Tasks and Steps in an Activity	9
3	Mind Map	31
4	Project Outline	33
5	Project Flowchart	34
6	Completed Example of Workform 2: Estimate of Productive Work Hours Available	41
7	Existing Data Example	45
8	Completed Example of Workform 3: Determining Who Does What	48
9	Completed Example of Workform 4: Standard Terms in Our Library for Tasks and Steps	50
10	Completed Example of Workform 5: Analysis of Staff Time: Work Unit Estimate of Time Spent on Activities	54
11	Completed Example of Workform 6: Analysis of Staff Time: Individual Estimate of Time Spent on Activities	55
12	Completed Example of Workform 7: Recording Staff Tasks: Self-Report Log	56
13	Completed Example of Workform 8: Recording Staff Tasks: Direct Observation Log	58
14	Ash Branch Workloads	59
15	Macroview of Building a Collection	63
16	Microview of Selecting Titles	64
17	Completed Example of Workform 9: Analysis of a Task (Observation)	67
18	Completed Example of Workform 10: Time Spent on an Input-Driven Task	71
19	Completed Example of Workform 11: Time Spent on a Demand-Driven Task	75
20	Ash Branch Workloads by Fiscal Year	78
21	Mean Circulation per FTE	79

22 Median Circulation per FTE   80

23 Percentage of Change   82

24 Graphic Comparison of Circulation   83

25 Ranking Numeric Results   85

26 Ranking Nonnumeric Factors   86

27 Completed Example of Workform 13:
        Workflow Chart   90

28 Flow Diagram of Task or Step Sequences   91

29 Flow Diagram of Technical Services Department   92

30 Plan, Do, Check, Act Cycle   109

Acknowledgments

The authors would like to thank the members of the *Staffing for Results* team for their enormous contribution to this book. The insights and experiences of Renee Blalock, Marilyn Boria, Rita Hamilton, Thomas Hehman, Luis Herrera, Susan Hildreth, Larry Price, and E. J. Woznick helped structure the process and define the concepts found here.

We also appreciate the staff at the Birmingham (Alabama) Public Library, the Baltimore County (Maryland) Public Library, and the Bedford (Virginia) Public Library for field testing the workforms.

June Garcia and Sandra Nelson have once again contributed their clear and compelling vision to another "Results" publication. Their guidance and leadership are invaluable.

Introduction

Managing a public library has always been hard work, and it is becoming even more difficult under the twin pressures of restricted public funding and rapid change. The Public Library Association (PLA) plays a major role in providing the tools and training required to "enhance the development and effectiveness of public librarians and public library services."[1] During the past five years, PLA has provided support for the development of a family of management publications that are being used by library managers, staff, and boards around the country to manage the libraries in their communities more effectively. The publications are

Planning for Results: A Public Library Transformation Process

The New Planning for Results: A Streamlined Approach

Managing for Results: Effective Resource Allocation for Public Libraries

Wired for the Future: Developing Your Library Technology Plan[2]

Staffing for Results: A Guide to Working Smarter

These five documents provide a fully integrated approach to planning and resource allocation, an approach that is focused on creating change—on *results.* The underlying assumptions in all five publications are the same:

Excellence must be defined locally. It is a result of providing library services that match community needs, interests, and priorities.

Excellence does not require unlimited resources. It occurs when available resources are allocated in ways that support library priorities.

Excellence is a moving target. The best decision-making model is to estimate, implement, check, and adjust—and then estimate, implement, plan, and adjust again.

The "Results" Publications

The first publication in the family was *Planning for Results: A Public Library Transformation Process*. It was replaced in 2001 by *The New Planning for Results: A Streamlined Approach*. Both of these books describe a library planning process that is focused on creating an actual blueprint for change rather than a beautifully printed plan for your office shelf. As you can see in the following diagram of the *Planning for Results* model, the process starts by looking at the community the library serves to identify what needs to happen to improve the quality of life for all of the community's residents. Once the community's needs have been established, library planners look for ways the library can collaborate with other government services and not-for-profit agencies to help meet those needs. That, in turn, provides the information required to establish the library's service priorities.

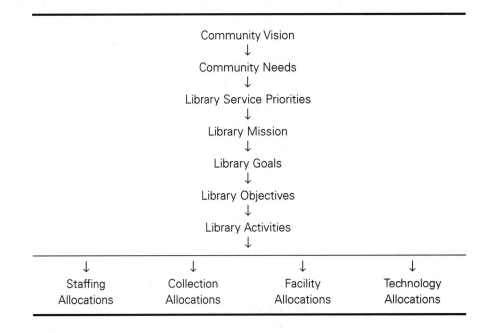

The planning process includes significant participation by community residents who represent all of the constituencies served by the library: parents and children, working adults and seniors, business people and civic leaders, students and educators, the various ethnic and religious groups in your community, government and not-for-profit leaders, and all of the other groups that together create your unique community. By involving all of these groups in your planning process you ensure that the services you provide are really what community residents want—and not what you or your staff or board think (or wish) that they want.

Because *The New Planning for Results* is focused on identifying and implementing the activities that will help library managers and staff accomplish community-based goals and objectives, the decisions that are made are sure to affect every part of library operations. In the past, some library managers have considered planning to be about identifying new services and programs, with the unspoken but very real assumption that their current services and programs were "just fine, thank you very much." That is no longer a viable option. There have been too many changes in the past decade, and there are too many new audiences to serve, too many new services to provide, and too many new tools available to provide them. No library is going to get enough new dollars to make all these needed changes. Our only option is to reallocate existing resources to provide new and evolving services.

Every library manager, staff member, and board member must get used to the idea of continuously evaluating all of the services and programs the library currently provides in the context of the library's identified priorities—and then be willing to make changes when the two don't match. Changes don't happen because we want them to or hope they will; changes only happen when we do things differently. The remaining three books in the PLA "Results" family provide library managers with the practical tools they need to decide which things to do differently and how to make the needed changes. They help managers to determine what resources will be required to actually implement the activities selected during the planning process.

Managing for Results

Managing for Results: Effective Resource Allocation for Public Libraries is a primer for managers and provides the basic tools they need to help them make more effective resource allocation decisions. It presents an overview of resource allocation issues in public libraries as well as an introduction to the specific issues to be considered when looking at the four main library resources: staff, collections, facilities, and technology. It includes a selection of fifty-six workforms to help you gather the data you need to make informed resource allocation decisions—and strongly encourages that you be very selective when using those forms. The general rule is "do not collect any data that you don't plan to use in the immediate future."

Managing for Results provides a considerable amount of information in a single volume—which is both its strength and its weakness. On the positive side, everything that you need to begin making data-based resource allocation decisions is available in that one volume. The fact that information is presented about all four major library resources makes it easier to understand the interrelationship among the four—and very few activities affect just a single resource. On the other hand, when you start reading about all of the issues surrounding all of the resource allocation decisions that library managers are facing today, the whole process can seem overwhelming.

Even though at first glance *Managing for Results* appears to include more information than most of us think we will ever use, the book is intended to provide an overview of resource allocation issues and basic tools for considering each of the four resource areas. This makes *Managing for Results* an excellent place to start the process of making data-based resource allocation decisions. However, when you delve into *Managing for Results* and actually begin using the recommended processes and forms, you will probably find occasions when you need more-detailed data-gathering tools or more help with analyzing the data you have collected. The following publications provide the extended coverage you need in the areas of technology and staffing.

Wired for the Future

Wired for the Future: Developing Your Library Technology Plan was written to help library managers make decisions about establishing a technological infrastructure and select products and services to support that infrastructure. It was used by many libraries to make the decisions required by the E-Rate process and the first round of Gates Foundation grants (which seem to be ancient history for most of us now but were challenging and even traumatic for many of us the first time we dealt with them). *Wired for the Future* is fully compatible with *Planning for Results*—the library's service priorities serve as a starting point for the decisions to be made when establishing a technology infrastructure just as they do for every other resource allocation decision.

Wired for the Future provides considerably more detailed information about the allocation of technology resources than does *Managing for Results*. If your library infrastructure needs to be significantly upgraded or changed, you will probably want to use *Wired for the Future* as the basis for your decision making. If, on the other hand, your library's basic technological infrastructure is in place and your resource allocation decisions are going to be based on the availability and use of your existing hardware, software, and online resources, then *Managing for Results* has the tools that you need.

Staffing for Results

Staffing for Results can be used by library managers and staff to identify and collect the information they need to make informed staffing decisions and to monitor the results of those decisions. The workforms will help you gather data so that you can analyze tasks and measure staff workloads. The narrative sections will help you interpret what you have measured and determine what additional data, if any, is needed to make decisions.

The chapter on staffing in *Managing for Results* "is intended to help managers determine the staffing required and identify the abilities needed to accomplish the library's service goals, objectives, and activities." *Managing for Results* provides an overview of the issues to be addressed when considering staff allocations and reallocations and a selection of workforms to help begin the process of analyzing what will be needed to accomplish the library's service priorities. In general, the materials in *Managing for Results* start at the service priority level and provide some guidance for working at the activity level. The information in *Staffing for Results,* on the other hand, starts at the activity level and provides considerable support for evaluating workloads at the task level.

The materials in these two books are fully compatible. The difference is one of depth. *Managing for Results* has the tools you need to decide if significant changes in staffing patterns will be required to accomplish your library's service priorities. If you decide that major staff adjustments will be required, you may need to use the tools in *Staffing for Results* to decide exactly what changes you should make and what the ramifications of those changes would be. This mirrors the relationship between using *Managing for Results* and using *Wired for the Future* for technology decisions.

Some Basic Definitions

Before you begin to read this book and use its suggestions and workforms to make staffing decisions, it will be helpful if you understand how some basic terms have been used. Every public library is a little different. Staff in one library talk about "branches," in another library the term is "agencies," and in a third staff refer to both branches and departments as "units." Some libraries have "central" libraries, others have "main" libraries. There are libraries that report to governing boards and libraries that are units of the government entity that funds them, which may or may not have advisory boards. These differences can cause confusion among readers because each reader expects to see his or her reality reflected in the terms and examples used. A list of terms and their meanings *in this book* follows:

> *branch*—a separate facility
>
> *central library*—the largest library facility, usually in a downtown area; referred to as the main library in some places
>
> *department*—a unit within a single facility that is usually a central library
>
> *library*—the entire organizational entity and its units

manager—a generic term that refers to the staff member who is responsible for resource allocation in a particular area; in some libraries the "manager" is actually a team of staff members

team—a group of staff members brought together to work on a specific project or program; often includes members from different departments and with different job classifications

unit—a term used to refer to library departments and branches, if any

The Tree County Public Library

Previous books in the "Results" family include case studies based on the Anytown Public Library, a single facility with no branches that provides bookmobile services throughout the county. *Staffing for Results* introduces a new fictional library, the Tree County Public Library. Tree County is a mythical county somewhere in the United States with a countywide population of 400,000 people. The library serves the residents of Tree County with seven branches and has a governing board.

How to Use This Book

Staffing for Results is divided into six chapters and thirteen workforms. Chapter 1 introduces the basic concepts of workload analysis and defines many of the terms used throughout the book. It provides information on the types of problems and management challenges that can be addressed with workload analysis. It also discusses ways to communicate with staff about workload analysis projects and processes.

Chapter 2 presents information on developing a plan to conduct a workload study. Workload analysis can be frightening to staff who have never participated in such an activity before. They often see it as a direct assault on the quality of their work, and they fear that the outcome of such a study will be increased work expectations or punitive measures based on poor performance numbers.

Chapter 3 describes one of the two basic ways to measure workloads: numeric analysis. It provides information on assessing the data you presently collect for its usefulness in workload analysis. It also describes three ways in which you can develop additional data to complete numeric analyses.

Chapter 4 focuses on the other basic way to measure workloads: process analysis, the technique of determining the steps taken to produce a measurable output such as cataloging materials or answering reference questions. It also contains information on the types of work done in libraries and discusses how data gathering differs for public service and technical or administrative functions.

Chapter 5 introduces advanced data analysis techniques. A range of numeric calculations are explained, and information is provided on how to select the most relevant calculation for your information needs. Work-flow mapping and delay identification are discussed in this chapter also.

Finally, chapter 6 covers how to act on what you learn. This book emphasizes over and over again that there is no point in measuring workloads if you don't intend to act on what you learn. Communicating results, engaging staff, dealing with resistance, and implementing change are the focuses of this chapter.

Staffing for Results will help library managers and boards deploy their staff resources effectively to implement the library's goals and objectives. That clearly implies that before managers and board members can use this book effectively, they must have a clear understanding of what they are trying to accomplish. This book is a part of PLA's "Results" publications, so there are references throughout the book to library planning documents developed using the *New Planning for Results* process. However, that certainly is not the only process that libraries use to identify priorities. Some libraries have participated in city or county strategic planning processes. Other libraries chose to develop annual goals and objectives for the library as a whole rather than developing a multiyear plan. Yet others developed goals and objectives for individual units or for specific programs or services.

Even libraries that do not go through any kind of formal planning process have implicit plans that are reflected in their budgets. In fact, no matter what planning process a library uses, the budget identifies the actual priorities that will be addressed during the fiscal year. Although the budget reflects the library's final priorities, there are two main problems with using the budget-development process as the primary library planning mechanism. First, it is easy to let the available resources determine what services will be provided rather than building the service program on identified community needs. In other words, the tail often wags the dog. Second, using the budget as your principal planning tool makes it very easy to continue existing programs and fairly difficult to reallocate existing resources for new programs.

What should you do if your library has no current plan other than your budget? Must you complete a whole planning process before you can use any of the tools in this book? Absolutely not. *Staffing for Results* can be used to make staffing decisions regardless of your environment. However, it is worth repeating that this book is about implementing priorities and not about determining what those priorities should be. *Before you can decide how to deploy your staff effectively you must know what you want to accomplish.* Any process used to determine the library's desired outcomes can serve as the starting point for the processes described in this book.

Sandra Nelson

NOTES

1. Public Library Association Mission Statement. Available at http://www.pla. org/factsheet.html on 9/7/01.

2. Ethel Himmel and William James Wilson, *Planning for Results: A Public Library Transformation Process* (Chicago: American Library Assn., 1998); Sandra Nelson, *The New Planning for Results: A Streamlined Approach* (Chicago: American Library Assn., 2001); Sandra Nelson, Ellen Altman, and Diane Mayo, *Managing for Results: Effective Resource Allocation for Public Libraries* (Chicago: American Library Assn., 2000); Diane Mayo and Sandra Nelson, *Wired for the Future: Developing Your Library Technology Plan* (Chicago: American Library Assn., 1999).

Chapter 1

Keys to Success

MILESTONES

By the time you finish this chapter you will know how to

- determine ways in which you can use workload analysis in making data-based decisions

- anticipate the types of issues that arise in a workload analysis project

- communicate effectively with staff about workload analysis

- form an advisory group to assist with large or complex workload analysis projects

Library services and the work that staff do to deliver them are changing so rapidly that it's hard to keep up. New tasks are added to staff responsibilities to get the job done. So many things have "the highest priority" that inevitably some tasks don't get done. Everyone is looking for help in accomplishing what seems like an ever-growing amount of work.

Library personnel costs are a significant and growing part of any library's budget. Justifying added staff positions or hours is not an easy process because library directors and managers compete with other departments within their governmental jurisdictions or with other units in the library for budget dollars. Reallocating budgeted hours or positions is also a challenging activity. Demand for a service rarely falls away completely, which means difficult choices have to be made and political support has to be developed for these choices. In addition to the political acumen necessary to finesse these changes, library managers need solid data and analysis to support the bases of their decisions.

Many library managers rely upon their experience and intuition in making resource allocation decisions. While often incisive, such a decision-making process can be hard for other managers and staff to follow and understand. The techniques provided in this book can be used to bolster and reinforce a manager's intuitive conclusions and can be regarded as another set of tools to add to the effective manager's toolbox. Developing expertise in using these techniques will allow staff and managers at all levels to complement subjective gut instincts with data-driven analyses and recommendations.

Your first reaction may be to dismiss the data gathering and analysis recommended in this book as too time-consuming, too difficult, or even inappropriate for a public service institution like a public library. "Bean counters" are typically regarded as heartless, bottom-line driven functionaries who don't value the nuances of responsive service delivery. Some staff complain that focusing on numbers (defined by them as sheer quantity) disregards issues of service quality and substance.

However, studying work processes and workloads doesn't invalidate your intuition. Sound data collection and analysis can provide insights that reliance upon experience (which, by definition, is based on the past) or leaps of intuition cannot. While those closest to the work should be turned to for ideas regarding processes and improvements, they are often limited by their own preconceived ideas and assumptions about how things are done. Objective analysis of the components of the work being studied offers everyone the opportunity to look at the work and work processes in ways that are different from their ingrained perspectives.

These techniques also provide a mechanism for going beyond describing what is happening to finding the reasons. Most library workers perform a number of tasks, and often the same tasks are performed by a number of workers. Identifying what work is being done, by whom, and in what manner will provide information that can be used both diagnostically and therapeutically. In other words, just understanding all the steps and people involved in the work you are analyzing may cause you to say, "Ah ha, I see the problem. Now that I see it, I can fix it."

Alternatively, you may say, "I see that there is something going on here, but I don't know why. I need to do another round of data gathering to see if I can find out why there are differences among the work units." This situation usually requires the involvement of others to generate ideas that can be pursued as possible causes for the information uncovered. Asking additional questions, developing hypotheses, and then gathering more data to test your hypotheses is a mining process. You dig deeper until you find the answer to your question.

Work Is Changing

Traditional library measures, such as number of items circulated or reference questions answered, appear to be stable or declining in some libraries. However, staff members seem more stressed than ever before. The connection between these measures and staff perception of the workload is broken. If you are reading this book it is probably because you are trying to respond to these staff concerns.

Perhaps you have noticed the disconnect between work as measured by traditional statistics and staff perceptions and aren't sure on what basis you should respond. The traditional measures of library work obviously don't reflect all of the activities and tasks in a modern library. The stress and pressure staff feel is directly related to this issue: They feel that the work they're doing isn't being counted, recognized, or fully understood—and they are probably right.

Work is changing in libraries. What was once regarded as "traditional" library work is evolving into an entirely different picture of the work. For example, reference librarians find themselves working less behind a reference desk and more as trainers and instructors (both formally in classroom settings and informally as they work individually with library users) or as Web-content developers. Children's librarians are spending more time outside library facilities delivering materials to child-care centers, providing instruction or book talks in schools, or working with other community agencies that serve children.

Library work is changing in another significant way, too. For years, the bulk of public library work involved circulating library materials, answering questions at public desks, providing some programming for children, and selecting library materials. Few specialists got involved in the more arcane aspects of ordering and cataloging materials, and even fewer became involved in working with the library's automated circulation and online cataloging system. Now, activities, tasks, and areas of specialization have proliferated. Libraries of all sizes find themselves involved in public relations and marketing activities. Accounting and budgeting have become more sophisticated, as have human relations and other aspects of library management. Library automation has grown well beyond an automated circulation system. Libraries are now challenged to find and employ technology specialists who can integrate the automated library systems with desktop computers and local and wide area networks.

The public's expectation of library service is changing as well. People want more and different services than they did ten years ago. Library users expect to find a variety of media formats on the shelves along with the books. They expect computers as well as study carrels. They want staff to assist them with or train them in navigating the world of electronic information and the Internet. These changing expectations mean that staff have to master new skills and use those skills in delivering services.

Although each of these changes involves work that can be measured, that work is not being measured in many libraries. These are relatively new areas, and ways to measure the work related to them have not been established or, in some cases, defined. However, substantial portions of the library's overall workload are taking place in these non-traditional areas. Library managers may be interested in determining how much of their staff members' time is being devoted to these activities by asking the same sorts of questions about the new activities that are asked about the more traditional library activities.

Staff Time—A Limited Resource

The most common complaint of staff is that there isn't time to get all of the work done. Mastering new skills, supporting new or expanded services, and keeping up with all of the traditional services at the same time is impossible. It is important to remember that most library staffs are not sitting around with extra time on their hands. Staffs are fully employed doing the jobs they were hired to do. To add to those jobs or change them significantly means changing the way staffs allocate the hours of their days. It means doing some tasks in less time *(operating more efficiently)* or dropping some tasks altogether to make time for new tasks *(operating more effectively)*.

Efficiency means "doing things right," and *effectiveness* means "doing the right things." Efficiency and effectiveness are not natural outcomes of daily operations. They require effort to achieve and regular monitoring to maintain. They are also constantly moving targets. Efficiency is affected both by the ways things are done and by the available tools. Effectiveness is based on doing those things that will result in achieving the library's goals. As a library's service goals evolve, so, too, does the determination of which tasks are most effective in supporting those goals.

Distributing work among staff is one of the most challenging tasks in an organization. It raises issues of reasonable expectations, fairness, and organizational values. Everyone wants to feel that the tasks they are assigned are important in accomplishing the library's goals and are valued by the organization. Everyone also wants to feel that the people around them are pulling their fair share of the load. However, some staff members feel they are being asked to work harder than others, or they feel the tasks they have been assigned are not relevant to achieving the library's priorities as they understand them. How many times have you heard reference staff complain that helping people with Internet computers keeps them from doing their "real" work of answering reference questions?

As important as task assignments and staffing levels are, most decisions about them are made on gut feeling, not on data. Faced with staffing decisions, most managers do what seems right. For example, if one branch has two children's staff and five staff for adults, and that seems to work, they'll staff the new similarly sized branch that way too. If one library with an annual circulation of 200,000 gets its materials shelved within 24 hours with X number of full-time library pages, other libraries with similar circulations and staffing should be as efficient, or so the reasoning goes. It's not that library managers want to operate on feelings, but most just don't have any readily available data to base their decisions on.

CASE STUDY	When the Tree County Public Library completed its strategic plan last year, Current Topics and Titles was selected as a top service response. The materials budget was increased by 10 percent from $500,000 to $550,000, with the increase earmarked to expand the nonprint collection, which was the portion of the library's circulating collection with the highest turnover. The increased expenditure means the library will be able to double the number of nonprint materials it buys.
TREE COUNTY PUBLIC LIBRARY TECHNICAL SERVICES	

When the Tree County Public Library completed its strategic plan last year, Current Topics and Titles was selected as a top service response. The materials budget was increased by 10 percent from $500,000 to $550,000, with the increase earmarked to expand the nonprint collection, which was the portion of the library's circulating collection with the highest turnover. The increased expenditure means the library will be able to double the number of nonprint materials it buys.

The technical services department head worries about her staff's ability to absorb the increase. The department has a staff of five: two full-time cataloger/database-maintenance staff, one acquisitions person, one processing and mail clerk, and a paraprofessional who works half time on the database and half time in acquisitions. The department has no significant backlogs of materials to be processed, and the department head doesn't want to create one now that the budget has been increased to buy more popular materials.

She takes her concerns to the director, who asks how much additional staff would be needed. The department head suggests that a 10 percent increase in materials requires a 10 percent increase in staff, which seems reasonable to the director. Adding a .5 FTE (full-time equivalent) staff member, or a staff member for 20 hours a week, to technical services provides that 10 percent increase. The director is committed to increasing the circulation by providing more popular materials and agrees to find 20 hours a week from other areas that could be assigned to technical services at the start of the new budget year.

Does this scenario sound familiar to you? Lacking actual data about how long it takes to process nonprint materials, the head of technical services guesses 20 hours a week will be enough. If the nonprint circulation increases by 20 percent when the new materials arrive on the shelves, someone in public services will guess that a 20 percent increase in shelving hours will be needed to reshelve the materials. Will these solutions avoid future problems? You will revisit Tree County in later chapters to see how well "gut reaction" decision making really works.

Staffing decisions are made like this every day in libraries, based on guesses. With some data to support your decision making, you can turn your guesses into reasonable estimates.

Decisions Require Data

Many library managers would argue that their intuitive decisions are not guesses but are based on experience and knowledge about their library and its operations. Experienced managers have a "mental model" of the services their organization offers and the staffing and other resources needed to provide those services. This internalized view helps them cope with the myriad decisions they are called upon to make every day.

However, every mental model needs regular updating, and intuition and gut feelings are not defensible outside the library. As public agencies face continuing pressure to control costs and demonstrate value, funding requests and budgets need to be supported by data. Traditional library statistics reflect only a portion of a modern library's activities. Tasks such as Internet training, PC support, and Web-site maintenance are rarely counted or reported. We need better data to explain or project our staffing needs. We need better data to update our own mental models so we can develop an accurate understanding of the work processes and service demands within our own institutions.

Even the traditional statistics can hide significant changes in workloads. Consider a library with stable circulation numbers where the proportion of materials on hold has dramatically increased as the result of patron-placed holds. Handling such holds is much more labor intensive than checking out a book the patron found on the shelf. The materials need to be trapped at check-in or retrieved from the shelves, then transported from the branch where they are trapped to the pickup branch and placed on holding shelves awaiting pickup. The patron needs to be notified, and staff need to retrieve the materials for checkout when the patron comes in. In this case the reported circulation statistics may look stable, but the workload associated with those numbers (the patron-placed holds) is greatly increased.

As library managers and staff struggle with the changes all libraries are undergoing, making informed decisions is crucial. We have a finite set of resources to work with, especially staff resources. We need to use those resources as effectively and efficiently as we can. Staff members need to focus their work on the activities that are most directly related to achieving the library's goals, and activities that do not contribute to accomplishing those goals need to be identified and eliminated. Extraneous steps in necessary procedures need to be pruned. As services are changed or new services are introduced, we need to monitor the effects on workloads, looking at planned and unplanned results.

This book will help you identify and collect the information you need to make informed decisions and to monitor the results of those decisions. The workforms and instructions at the end of the book will help you analyze tasks and measure staff workloads. The factors to consider in the instructions for each workform will help you interpret what you measure and determine what additional data you might need to make decisions. Understanding the workloads in your library will help you and your staff make better, more effective use of the time available to deliver service and achieve the library's goals.

What Is Workload Analysis?

Workload analysis will help you understand the processes whereby work is accomplished in your library. Work can be analyzed using two methods. *Numeric analysis* measures the number of outputs (see definition following) produced with a particular level of effort to develop numeric standards that will allow you to monitor performance on an ongoing basis through periodic measurements and statistical analyses. *Process analysis* studies the process itself and looks for ways to redesign the process through reordering, changing, or eliminating steps in the process to improve performance.

Following are some terms used when discussing workload analysis throughout this book:

An *activity* is composed of a set of tasks that results in a measurable output of things done or services delivered.

Baselines measure the current levels at which work is performed and outputs are produced.

Effort is the amount of time a person expends in creating an output.

Inputs are the materials, people, information, and environmental conditions needed to carry out a task or activity.

A *longitudinal study* is a comparison of several sets of numeric measures collected over time to determine if there are any significant changes in the numbers.

Numeric measures are calculations of the number of outputs produced per unit of effort.

Outputs are the measurable results from an activity, such as the products or services that are handed off to the customer.

Performance assessment or *performance monitoring* is the process of measuring work outputs and the in-process parameters that affect outputs.

Performance measures are standards against which numeric measures can be compared for evaluation purposes.

Steps are the sequential actions taken in the performance of a task.

A *task* is composed of a series of steps that converts inputs to an output.

A *trend* is a progressive increase or decrease in measured data, that is, a nonrandom change in the results.

Understanding the relationship between activities, tasks, and steps is key to using the tools provided in this book. Figure 1 provides a graphic representation of the relationship between these three key terms. Figure 2 shows an example of a set of tasks and steps within the activity of cataloging.

Activities, tasks, and steps are the three levels at which you can study work. You can develop numeric measures at all three levels. Process analysis takes place at the task and step levels.

Numeric Analysis

At its simplest, numeric analysis helps you determine how much you are getting done with the staff you have. Specifically, numeric analysis

FIGURE 1

Activity/Task/Step Relationship

	ACTIVITY		
Task	Task	Task	Task
Step 1	Step 1	Step 1	Step 1
Step 2	Step 2		Step 2
Step 3	Step 3		
	Step 4		

FIGURE 2

Example of a Set of Tasks and Steps in an Activity

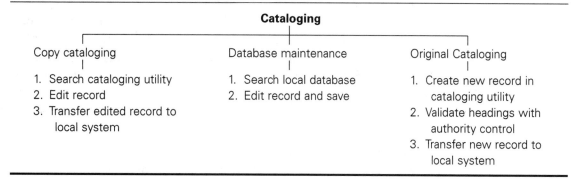

FIGURE 2

Example of a Set of Tasks and Steps in an Activity

calculates the number of outputs (products or services delivered) produced by a specific level of effort (employee time). The result is the workload.

$$\text{Workload} = \frac{\text{Output}}{\text{Effort}}$$

Numeric measures can range from the very general (average number of books circulated per staff hour) to the very specific (number of steps and minutes needed to process each new videotape). As you move from studying activities to studying tasks and from tasks to steps, your numeric measures will become more precise. They will also take more time and effort to gather and analyze.

Numeric measures themselves are simply snapshots of what is being done at the time the data is collected. Analyzing and interpreting numeric measures makes them useful in decision making. Periodic numeric measurement provides library staffs with the opportunity to evaluate their progress in achieving some of their goals, particularly if those goals include standards for performance measurement.

Numeric measures can be used to establish performance-measurement baselines and monitor conformity with those baselines. Baseline measures can aid in allocating staff resources among branches, departments, or services, or they can provide a basis for projecting staff needs for planned activities. To achieve any of these purposes you will need to gather data, perform some calculations and analysis, and then interpret what you find. Setting baselines might be possible with the data you are collecting today, but you may find, as one library director said, "I have looked over our statistics, and I don't see too much that is relevant."

Numeric measures can also help you assess changes in performance over time or determine the costs of various activities. To use numeric measures as a trend-spotting or problem-solving tool, you will need to collect and analyze data. As you track down a problem, your analyses will probably generate additional questions that will lead to further data collection. Numeric analyses often lead you back to doing a process analysis to clarify what the numbers are telling you. Workload analysis can be a very iterative process: every set of data seems to identify something else that could be investigated.

With careful attention to the details of what specifically is being measured, numeric measures *may* be comparable among different libraries, but such comparisons are very "soft" because the measurements are affected significantly by factors such as the starting and ending points of the measured work, the actual tasks included in the measured work, and unreported external environmental factors that affect the results.

Numeric measures are most relevant and valuable in comparing a library staff's performance with its own established baselines. Longitudinal studies, comparing one year's performance with prior or succeeding years, are one important use of numeric measures. Longitudinal studies allow you to see trends over time. They can demonstrate efficiencies you have achieved and highlight potential problem areas as they are developing.

Process Analysis

Process analysis identifies the steps your staff takes in producing an output for a customer. Every activity has a customer, someone who uses the output that results from the tasks and steps. Sometimes the customer is a member of the public, sometimes it is another department in the library, and sometimes it is another person in the same department, but there is always a customer to receive the output at the end of any activity. If there weren't a customer, why would you spend time on the activity?

Process analysis provides an opportunity for staff to identify problem points in a work flow, understand the factors that affect performance, and question why certain actions are taken. In analyzing a task, you determine what steps are taken and in what sequence they are performed to produce the output. Once you have identified the steps, you can begin to ask questions about them. Are these the right steps to produce this output? Are the steps performed in the right order? Is there duplication in the steps or something important that is being left out? Are there sufficient quality control checkpoints in the process or perhaps too many quality checks? Of course the key question in process analysis is always: "Does each step in this task add something to the output that increases the customer's satisfaction with the output?" If you can't answer yes, then you have found a task that is a prime candidate for redesign or elimination.

Sometimes just listing the steps in a task, or comparing the steps taken by various staff who are ostensibly doing the same work, is sufficient to identify ways in which you can improve organizational performance. You may find steps that were once necessary but are no longer important and, thus, can be eliminated. You may find that some staff have already found ways to eliminate steps without reducing quality, but their improvements have never been shared with others doing the same work. You may discover environmental factors, such as supplies that aren't conveniently located or tools that are shared, that can be changed to improve performance. Even seemingly small changes can make a big difference in performance, especially in tasks you perform hundreds or thousands of times each month.

Process analysis is a key tool in solving operational problems. If you have a backlog in technical services or reshelving, or a significant increase in the wait times at public services desks, you'll probably start your problem solving with process analysis to see what is actually going on and how the work is being performed.

Process analysis can be as general or as specific as you want it to be. You can increase the level of precision in a process analysis by narrowing your definition of the task and its steps. For example, you might define the activity of reference service as including the tasks of on-desk and off-desk work. The task of on-desk work might include the steps of direct public interaction, assistance with Internet PCs, and other desk work. In "other desk work" you include the myriad things that happen at a reference desk while staff are waiting for a customer to ask for help. To develop a more precise analysis, you might choose to designate "other desk work" as a task itself and define the steps as reading reviews, developing bibliographies, and planning programs. Each of these "steps" could in turn be studied as tasks with their own set of steps.

Beyond monitoring performance and solving problems, other possible uses for numeric measurements and process analysis include

> establishing staffing levels for new or existing facilities

> determining the number of service desks or delivery points (e.g., circulation checkout stations)

> determining minimum staffing levels for basic coverage

> addressing staffing allocation issues within or across branches or departments

> identifying the classification or level of staff required in a facility or work area

> developing baselines and best practices through performance and productivity monitoring as part of an ongoing performance assessment initiative

> determining if staff competencies are being used in the most effective manner

> developing arguments for increasing staffing levels

> uncovering underlying variables that cause differences among output measurements

discovering general trends in workloads

finding out how much time is needed to complete specific tasks

reviewing and analyzing the service mix and determining whether changes will be made in the offerings provided

Think about some of the decisions you have been called on to make recently. Would any of them have been easier if you had process or numeric data to base your decisions on?

Issues to Address

Studying workloads can be very disruptive in an organization. Staff will resent the implied criticism of their job performance. They will be concerned about how management will use the information it gathers, envisioning public comparisons among employees or annual personnel evaluations based solely on the numbers. In libraries with staff unions, a plan to study workloads may require meeting and conferring with the union before the process can begin.

Studying workloads doesn't necessarily result in identifying performance issues. However, let's be honest, sometimes that *is* what you find, and the staff know it. Expect to face resistance as you begin to study workloads and processes. The only way you will overcome the resistance is by communicating clearly and often why you are adding workload analyses to the data you gather and how you intend to use the information. Then do what you say you are going to do.

Internal Culture, Climate, and Values

Every library has its own culture, climate, and set of values. Public library employees are often very long-tenured and have built up tremendous organizational memory. Assumptions that people make about underlying motivations and hidden agendas are driven, to a great extent, by their own experiences and their memories and interpretations of them. These interpretations and memories can be quite faulty, but they are extremely powerful. Contemplating the established "mental models" held by individuals or groups in your library and their impact upon the planned workload analysis project—and preparing to provide information that can respond to them—will increase the likelihood of an effective project and greater receptivity to the recommendations that come out of it.[1]

Culture can refer to such things as the historical pecking order among staff classifications or between a central library and the branches. The culture may be that employees perceived as not being "people people" will ultimately end up in technical services. It may be that the culture decrees that librarians who specialize in serving children are not as highly regarded as those who serve primarily adults in a subject department of the main library. Cultural issues can also extend to such things as unwritten, unarticulated but tacitly agreed-upon assumptions about the appropriate amount of time to spend on a public service desk, the appropriate way to serve library users (take them to an area instead of pointing to it, for example), the appropriate way to serve children (*only* in the designated children's area), or the comfort level about the number of people lined up in front of a public service desk. Your workload analysis project will be taking place within your own library's culture, so acknowledging that it exists and working to understand (and possibly modify) it is important to the success of the project.

Climate relates to the general level of morale within the library employee group or groups and how included, supported, and valued employees feel. Some library systems have experienced decades of ill will between rank-and-file employees and management or the top administrative layer. A climate of distrust, suspicion, and cynicism prevails in such an organization. In other libraries, there is a general climate of trust and optimism and the assumption of good intent even in situations where the proposals of management raise questions. The approach taken to communication and problem solving should be adjusted depending upon the climate in which the project is taking place.

Values are intertwined with culture and climate. Values are the beliefs people have about what is good or worthwhile. It's a rare library employee who will say that he doesn't value providing good customer service, but the definitions and the means of achieving this end can vary widely. A circulation clerk, for example, can assert that good customer service means that no one has to wait in line to be served. A library manager might assert that people wait in lines at the supermarket and at the post office, so why can't they wait in lines for a reasonable period of time at the library? The manager's idea of good customer service might be to tolerate lines to a certain extent so that clerical time can be used to get the daily newspaper out more quickly in the morning. Who's right? How would we know?

Communicating Effectively

Remember the old realtors' saying that the most important three factors in selecting a home are location, location, and location? The importance of communication in a workload analysis project (or any major project) could be stated in the same emphatic way.

It seems universal that public library directors as well as their employees cite "communication" as a central problem or concern. When a project hits as close to the bone of income and the value placed on one's work as workload analysis does, it's even more important that all aspects of the project, from the reason for it to what will be done with the results, are thoroughly communicated to library employees.

The employees whose work is being measured *must* be involved. It's also advisable to inform the rest of the staff so that they know what the project is about, why a particular work group or activity is being measured, and what that might mean to others on the staff as well. Effective communication requires not only that a message be sent but that the sender understand it. It also requires that the receiver not only receive the message but also understand it and be affected by it. It's important to consider the kinds of communications issues that might arise, approaches to addressing those issues, and the vehicles that could be used to communicate with staff.[2]

Information Needs

At the most basic level, staff need to know what the study is all about: Why is the project being done? Who will be involved? How will it be done? What will be done with the results? The staff charged with the execution of the workload analysis project can help generate these questions, provide succinct and informative answers, and distribute this information to the rest of the library staff.

A variety of different vehicles should be used to communicate to staff about the project. Special topic newsletters, question-and-answer information sheets, memos, e-mail distributions, and intranet sites are all effective ways of getting this information out. Whatever method or combination of methods is used, be sure to include who is involved in the project, what each person's role is, and whom to contact for more information. Write in a friendly, accessible manner rather than a terse, bureaucratic fashion. If potential trouble areas or hot spots have been identified, be honest in addressing them so that employees know that you are aware of the issues and what is being done to resolve them.

As the project progresses, share progress reports, project-team minutes, and other relevant information with the staff. If problems arise that adversely impact the time line, let staff know that the project has been delayed, not derailed. Even if there is no real news to relay, let the staff know that the project is underway and that information will be shared with them at a future time. Without reassurance, the vacuum will be filled with rumor and suppositions, which will probably be quite untrue.

Studies have shown that employees value one-on-one, face-to-face communication most highly. While it often isn't practical to use this as the only communication vehicle, it is important that the project manager and the library's senior managers communicate in person at least occasionally. Talking with people allows them to connect with you and with the project. It provides an opportunity to demonstrate your authentic interest in the individuals and in their reactions to the project. Investing the time to meet with employees who will be directly involved in the measurement project will pay off in both the short and long run. You'll hear their questions and concerns and get a sense of how effective the data gathering may be by their receptivity. They will see you as directly connected to the project and know that you care enough about them to come and talk to them about it. The project will seem more real if they are involved rather than being given a disembodied assignment through a memo or e-mail or a subordinate manager.

Communication Methods

Remember that multiple communications will be necessary. What is vitally important to you right now is hardly a blip on the screen of most of your fellow library employees. They'll probably have to hear about the project several times before they readily remember what it's about. Because the very nature of the project is something that can feel threatening and, thus, can be misunderstood, it makes sense to be very sensitive to the importance of providing ample information about it.

In many libraries, the informal grapevine is the fastest, most effective, and preferred communications mechanism. Don't fight it. Figure out how to harness it so you can get your message out. Team members can be instrumental in using such unofficial communications modes. Often a question-and-answer document is a useful tool because it allows you to capture a number of basic questions and concerns and answer them in a straightforward way. This method acknowledges the questions that are on staff minds, demonstrates that you know of them, and provides a simple vehicle for providing answers and context.

Whatever vehicles you choose, follow these basic rules:

Keep it simple—direct, concise, and without jargon.

Acknowledge whatever "soft issues" you are aware of. These are likely to be the issues that relate to climate, culture, and values. Say, "While our practice has been to have two librarians on the reference desk all hours the library is open, we're going to have to examine that practice in light of this year's budget cut."

Use examples or tell stories that relate to the real world of library work. Don't say, "We want to optimize our multicultural competencies." Say, instead, "We want to be sure that families who come to our libraries feel welcome and have someone to talk to who understands them."

Repeat and link back—remind staff that you told them about this before, that this is a progress report on a project that they've heard about before, that this is the final report on the project, etc. Let them know that the project relates to preparing to open the new Southside Branch in October of next year. It may seem obvious to you, but to the clerk who is trying to keep up with unpacking the delivery, it isn't going to be obvious.

Every time you communicate tell people whom to contact with questions or with more information. List the names and contact information for the project team members as well as for the project manager so that staff can contact them if that's their preference.

Forming an Advisory Group

An effective way to plan and manage a complex workload project or to deal effectively with a difficult communication environment is to form an advisory group of employees to assist with the project. Such a group can be helpful in a number of ways. It can

involve from the beginning employees who really know the work so that what is planned is relevant

flush out questions and concerns immediately so that they can be addressed as quickly as possible

identify, clarify, and help all to agree upon terms and concepts used by those doing the work under study so that information is gathered consistently and data can be readily compared across work units and locations

provide broad participation from the beginning to help in uncovering and addressing the fears and suspicions that are likely to be held by at least some staff members

sharpen your thinking and result in a more focused plan by talking with the group about the purpose of the workload analysis project

serve an important communications function within the organization because other staff may be more likely to ask advisory group members about the project and its implications than they would the library director or a manager, thus providing feedback from the front line back to the director or project manager in charge of the measurement effort

The advisory group can be involved in a number of ways: to develop the project, provide feedback and input at important junctures of the project, assist in analyzing project data and findings, actually carry out project implementation steps, or disseminate the project results throughout the library. However you decide to use the group, be sure you discuss their role and responsibilities with the group members and put the agreements reached in writing so that everyone knows and remembers what the group's charge is.

Depending upon the nature of the project, membership on the advisory group should include staff experts (from several locations if multiple locations are being studied) in the work that is to be done as well as supervisors or managers of the work areas under study. Take care to appoint a group that is respected and deemed knowledgeable by other library employees. Give consideration to differences that are already known among work units, and consider how these differences might have an impact on how work is organized and carried out. For example, if there are different sized branches or marked differences in busyness or very different service environments (for example, an inner city branch, a branch next door to a school, and a rural branch), take these differences into account as the representative group is fashioned.

Do It Only if You Will Use It

Workload analysis can be a continuous exercise in answering the question, "Why is this different?" However, few libraries have the luxury of time to investigate anomalies simply because they are interesting. Any workload study has to start with the end purpose in mind. Why do you need the information? What are you going to do with the results once you have them?

Use workload analysis to study work flows and performance problems only if you intend to make changes based on what you learn. What kind of changes? Studying workloads can help you

- do different things
- do things differently
- understand more thoroughly what work you do and the steps involved
- make work easier, smoother, or better for your staff

Staff are the most important of the four key resources available to accomplish a library's goals. (The other three are collections, facilities, and technology.) If you are planning to change the library's services to meet new or evolving customer needs, then staff will need to do different things with their days. Gathering data on workloads is one way to identify tasks that can be eliminated or streamlined to free up time.

Sometimes change isn't something you initiate, it is something you respond to. For example, a workload analysis of a shelving backlog could reveal a shift in customer usage patterns resulting in some library facilities checking in more items than they check out because the facility is in a convenient drop-off location. The changing proportion of print and nonprint materials that libraries circulate is another example of a shift in usage patterns to which a library must respond. It is easy to miss all of the impacts when activities are changed by external factors. Work flows that function well with one level of activity often break down under an increased load, but the problem has to build to a critical level before it is recognized.

Too often libraries respond to the warning signals of workload problems with workarounds or "temporary" solutions that become a permanent part of operations. If technical services gets backlogged, managers may decide to let branch staff put some of the labels on the materials instead of questioning the work flows in technical services. The next thing you know, branch staff are not only using labels supplied by technical services but also are creating and applying additional labels to support their own internal book-finding aids.

When backlogs begin to develop or deadlines start to be missed, workload analysis can help pinpoint the bottlenecks. With that information staff can redesign the work flow to accommodate the increased activity. Even changes you initiate can have unexpected consequences. Libraries that install self-charging machines usually expect that staff hours from the circulation desks can be reassigned since a portion of the work will migrate to the new machines. However, sometimes the expected reduction in needed hours doesn't materialize. Why? Although the number of staff/customer interactions is reduced, the length of each interaction increases because the proportion of customers at the desk with problems increases.

Workload analysis can also help identify ways in which work can be accomplished more easily. One library studying shelving performance found that its branches were simply too busy in the afternoons to permit shelving because book trucks in the aisles got in everybody's way. By switching the shelving activity to earlier in the day and using the afternoon hours for backroom work, productivity was improved.

Studying workloads also gives staff and managers an opportunity to assess the effectiveness of each step in the work, perhaps by identifying steps that were once important but that no longer contribute to the overall goals of the organization. Many library work flows were developed in paper-based environments and have not been redesigned in light of the automation libraries have installed in the last twenty years.

Changes in work processes don't have to be major disruptive organizational changes. There is often value in making continuous, small changes that over time build to major improvements in performance. Take small steps, evaluate the results and consequences, and then use that information to plan your next change. It will help everyone learn to manage and accept change. Also, it will help everyone see that workload analysis doesn't have to be threatening and that it can be a useful tool for making work more interesting, less repetitive, and more valued by your customers.

Making the Right Changes

Changes resulting from workload analysis are generally made after process analyses. Numeric analyses are diagnostic; they help you identify a problem. Process analyses are prescriptive; they help you determine what to do. The types of changes to processes that might result from a workload study include changes in

- who does the work
- where the work is done
- tools or materials used
- sources, types, or timing of inputs
- steps in the process
- outputs themselves

Staff and managers involved in process analyses that lead to redesigning work processes often worry about making the "right" decisions. How can you know that the changes you make will actually lead to the improvements you want, that you won't inadvertently end up making things worse? There is no magic way to guarantee that all of your decisions will be good ones, but there are some simple questions you can ask that will help you make choices. Consider the proposed changes and ask yourself the following questions:

Do they seem reasonable? Will other people in the organization agree that the changes being proposed will make a difference in the process being studied?

Is there a direct connection between the factors you are proposing to change and the process you are trying to affect?

Can you envision how things will look after the changes you are proposing take effect? Are there any consequences that you can foresee that might cause problems elsewhere in the organization? Is there anything you can do now to mitigate those consequences? If you can't or won't mitigate the expected consequences, at least acknowledge them and prepare for them.

What types of negative reactions do you expect the proposed changes to generate? How will you respond to those reactions? Some negativity results from people's discomfort with change, but some is generated by true concerns about the results of proposed changes. Think through the negative reactions you expect, and prepare your responses to them. This exercise will help you anticipate potential problems.

Introducing workload analysis into a library can be a challenge, but the rewards are well worth the effort. Setting baselines and testing performance against those baselines on a regular basis can identify emerging problems before they overwhelm the organization. Involving staff in workload analysis is a good way to solicit input on efficient operations from the folks who do the work. Being able to support budget requests with real data improves chances for success. Workload analysis can be an important tool in managing resources and achieving your library's service objectives.

Using This Book

The remaining chapters in this book will provide you with techniques and tools for conducting workload analyses. We suggest that you read through the book completely before you begin a workload analysis project. This will give you an overview of both numeric and process analyses and introduce the workforms provided to help you conduct your studies. After you understand the "big picture," you can return to those chapters that are most relevant to the study you intend to do.

There are thirteen workforms included in this book. These are designed to assist you in planning your workload analysis project and collecting the data you need to make decisions. Use only those workforms that you need to complete your planning and data gathering. Most projects will not use all of the workforms provided. Because of the iterative nature of workload analysis, the workforms you choose may not be used in numeric order, and a single workform may be used more than once throughout the course of a project.

NOTES

1. Mental models is one of the five disciplines of a learning organization. A very clear description of this concept, as well as exercises and tools such as "the ladder of inference," can be found in Peter M. Senge, et al., *The Fifth Discipline Fieldbook: Strategies and Tools for Building a Learning Organization* (New York: Doubleday, 1994), 235–93.

2. A very helpful explication of communication messages and mediums used in libraries is provided by Sandra Nelson in *The New Planning for Results: A Streamlined Approach* (Chicago: American Library Assn., 2001), 246–64.

Chapter 2

Design Your Project

MILESTONES

By the time you finish this chapter you will know how to

- set a goal for your workload analysis project

- identify possible trouble areas and develop plans to address them

- develop an outline, a sequence of tasks, and a time line for the project

- decide what type of data analysis you require

- determine the level of precision needed

Workload analysis projects are similar to other large-scale projects you and your colleagues have managed in the past. For example, most library managers have initiated a new service, participated in the planning for a new or remodeled facility, helped design the library's technological infrastructure, or managed grant programs. The skills you needed to successfully design and implement those projects are the same skills you will use when designing and implementing your workload analysis project.

The first—and most important—step to take when embarking on workload analysis is to carefully design the project. This starts by identifying why you are initiating the project. What problems do you want to solve or questions do you want answered? What purpose will the workload analysis project serve? How much data gathering will be required to accomplish your purpose? Who should be involved in designing and implementing the project? What communication processes need to be established to be sure that everyone in the library is informed throughout the project?

Sometimes library directors think that they can study workloads without involving staff or with just minor involvement by a supervisor or manager to help in gathering data. It's likely that this won't work. Employees are very sensitive to the interest in their work taken by the library director or other managers. They will note any changes in managerial behavior such as increased presence, questions and notes being taken in work areas, requests for additional statistics or information, etc. It's better to anticipate questions and err on the side of providing too much information rather than engendering even more suspicion about the process because people haven't heard from you what it's about.

Required Planning

Only the most basic "just-wondering" level of data review requires no planning and little or no involvement by others. While workload analysis can stop at this point, it's unlikely that it will, since *something* caused you to wonder in the first place. You could wonder, for example, about the comparative workload among circulation clerks in your branches or within the circulation unit in one building. If you find out that they all seem to be producing about the same amount of work, your question is answered, no additional data is required, and no change in methods or expectations is needed.

If your "just wondering" doesn't stop here, you're into a larger project. You'll need to ask more questions, gather more information, and seek help in interpreting the data you gather. Chapters 3 and 4 will help you define what type of data you want to collect and suggest ways to analyze that data. This chapter focuses on the all-important issues of planning the project and communicating with the staff about the workload analysis project.

Assumptions

As you begin formulating the workload analysis project in your mind and talking with others about it, start with these assumptions:

Only data needed for the project will be collected.

Something will be done with the data collected.

The data collected will probably generate a new set of questions.

You will stop when you've answered your questions.

There may be no absolute right or wrong answers.

Just asking the questions is value-laden and may provoke strong reactions.

Tough choices may be required.

You will need to communicate the results to the staff and other key stakeholders.

This probably won't be the only time you do this. It's a learning process; as you incorporate data gathering into your decision making, you will want to conduct workload analyses on a regular cycle.

These are potent assumptions. Discussing them and obtaining acceptance of them from others involved in the workload analysis project will be key to the project's positive reception and ultimate success.

Purpose

Your reason for undertaking a workload analysis probably links in some way to your current planning environment: goals in your strategic plan, new buildings, renovations, expansions or replacements in the master plan for your facilities, performance measures in your budget, or plans to extend or modify services or collections. If there is a clear linkage, explain it to library staff so that they see the workload analysis effort not as a new activity but as something that relates to and supports activities already underway.

The connection may not be so clear (for example, if you want to analyze backlogs or unsatisfactory time lags), or it may not really exist at all if the project is being done in reaction to external forces (a budget cut, for example). These issues do relate, however, to the overall mission of the library and the types and quality of services it performs. The point is to link the workload analysis activity with the larger plans, goals, services, and mission of the library so that library employees and managers see that gathering this information is designed to improve services to the library user. Because of the time and energy that workload analysis takes, everyone needs to feel that the end of improved or enhanced service justifies the means.

Plan to Plan

Once the purpose of the workload analysis project is clear in your mind, it's time to get additional input. Depending upon the size, structure, and culture of the organization, the initial discussion of the idea might begin between you and a manager or a first-line supervisor or with the employees involved in the work to be measured. Whatever the individual or group, the questions raised are likely to include the following:

- What is the workload analysis project all about?
- What is this *really* all about?
- Why do we need to do it?
- How will it be done?
- What will it mean to me? To my coworkers?
- Will it mean more work?
- Will I know how to do what you want? If not, will you train me?
- What will you do with what you find out?
- Who will decide what it means?
- Will you be judging me?
- Will jobs or hours be cut?
- Will I lose staff or be transferred?

Think through your answers to these questions before you begin talking about the project. You will encounter these questions (or slight variants of them) as you continue through the process. As you work with various groups and individuals, the answers will become refined and may, in fact, change. This fine-tuning is to be expected and welcomed in a collaborative planning and implementation process.

As you have these conversations, explore the following questions:

- What should be the criteria for success?
- How will we know if the project has answered our questions or fulfilled its purpose?
- How will we know we've come to the end?

These are critical questions to pose and answer. Write down the answers so that you can refer to them later on. It is surprising how often these significant points are forgotten or never really addressed. Disagreements, confusion, and disappointment are often the result when there are various definitions of success and the end point. This happens because there isn't agreement up front on what success and completion will look like.

If the library staff is unionized or represented by an employee group or association, involve the leadership in the project as early as possible. These staff leaders will be invaluable in surfacing issues, potential problems, and questions and in communicating to the staff the purpose and likely outcomes of the project. Failing to involve them almost signals that there is something for staff to worry about and raises the most negative theories regarding purpose and intent. Remember, "People are down on what they're not up on." Use all the communications mechanisms at your disposal, especially the ones that staff will automatically look to for information and protection.

Genuine involvement of employee leaders is key. If it's perceived that you're looking for easy buy-in or to co-opt them, suspicions and resentments will be even greater. Work to establish authentic dialogue so that you can receive questions and concerns that will help you craft an effective data gathering and evaluation process. Let's look at how the Tree County Public Library involved staff in planning a reference workload analysis.

CASE STUDY

TREE COUNTY PUBLIC LIBRARY REFERENCE SERVICES

Zeke Anders, reference head, has a problem—or at least he thinks he does. His staff tells him they are feeling more and more pressure and stress. He thought they'd be excited about the new public access PCs that provide Internet access and access to new electronic services and about getting the chance to show library users how to use them. Instead, all they do is complain. They say they didn't become librarians to clear paper jams, that they don't have time to help people, that people aren't using the computers for "real" library research. At the same time, he knows that the monthly reference statistics are down 20 percent in the last two years. How can the staff feel so busy when they are answering fewer reference questions? It doesn't seem that just looking at the statistics will be enough—certainly not enough to overcome all the griping he is hearing.

Zeke decides he needs to learn more about what is really happening at the reference desk. He talks it over with Mary Peterson, the library director, and she says to go ahead, but to be careful. "They're already riled up, Zeke. I don't want a grievance on my hands or another resignation. You know how hard it is to get good librarians these days."

Zeke decides to talk with the reference staff and broach the idea of finding out more about what is really taking place at the reference desk. He meets with department staff (both the librarians and support staff) and says he knows they are feeling pressured but that he is puzzled since the reference statistics are falling. Eyes begin to roll, so he hurries to add that he knows there is more to it than what the statistics represent. He says he wants to find out more about what is really taking their time. He asks for three volunteers from the department to work with him to figure out an approach to take. He makes a point of asking Myra, the union steward, if she will be one of the group since he values her expertise and feels she will be credible with the rest of the staff. He also knows that other staff members will ask her about what is really going on. Having Myra involved will forestall the wild speculation that always develops when something new is tried. He also makes sure that the project and its goals are described clearly in the reference department minutes since they are distributed throughout the library.

Preliminary discussion about the project should also take place with other individuals or groups who might be interested in the workload analysis project or who might be contacted with staff concerns. If the library is administratively answerable to a city or county manager, for example, that person should be briefed on the purposes and general scope of the study. If the library board is a governing board, they should be informed of the project.

Assistance with Project Design

If you decided to convene an advisory group for assistance with the project, use the members to help design the workload analysis project. Tell the group why you think it's necessary to undertake the project and what your goals for it are. Check out your basic hypotheses with them. Does what you propose make sense? Does the way you're thinking about doing the project seem likely to lead toward finding the information necessary to answer the questions you've posed? Are there questions that come to mind or that may come to the minds of their coworkers that need to be addressed? Even if your project is small and you aren't involving an advisory group, you should consider these questions, discuss them with others, and develop answers before you proceed.

Every organization's culture is different, so the starting point for this discussion and the pace at which it can be held will differ. For some libraries, doing such data gathering may be very new and might seem quite threatening. You might encounter questions every step of the way: "Why this?" "Why now?" "Why this way?" You might receive skeptical responses to what you think are straightforward answers. After all, you are wondering about the work that your employees are doing, raising questions about it, and all of the questions and concerns mentioned earlier can arise. The best advice is to go slow, remain patient, and explain clearly what you are trying to do and why. Don't expect everyone to take your responses at face value. If you've operated with integrity in the past, trust that most people will be willing to take the leap of faith with you in this instance also.

In other libraries, especially those with a history of using total quality management/continuous quality improvement techniques and tools, data gathering to analyze opportunities for service improvements or to improve processes will be standard operating procedure. In these libraries, the conversation will be less iterative and will move quickly to an experienced team of employees working on the best way to proceed in this particular data-gathering effort.

Assistance with Data Gathering

After you've clarified the purpose and potential outcomes of the project, develop the actual data-gathering steps and procedures. Again, be prepared to explain the rationale for your ideas and to answer questions that arise. Be prepared to make adjustments in methodology and schedule based on what you learn from the group.

Take full advantage of the advisory group's potential as advisors. You'll find as you proceed with this process that it is iterative and that there are points where questions will be raised, additional information will be gathered, and that, in turn, may lead to even more questions. These questions will include "What does this mean?" "What next?" and "Hmmm . . . what might account for these variations?" This is where staff expertise should be tapped and collectively explored. You might learn, for example, that an assumption that all circulation clerks do the same thing is false. You might find out how important it is to differentiate among the types of reference services offered at the desk because helping people search the Web takes considerably longer than just finding the answer for them.

Your understanding of the work that is being done will increase considerably. This increase in understanding will benefit you and the staff members on the advisory group as you become more adept at dissecting work processes and noting the impact of routines, space, and equipment. For example, one library found that awkward and time-consuming circulation routines could be traced back to a clerk with a broken arm and the accommodations that had been made for that person—and then became institutionalized for years.

Group members can also help determine the parameters of the study (the all-important stop point) and the parameters of the discussion about what it all means. Contemplation and speculation and theorizing could go on forever; it has to be pulled back to the initial purposes, and the group has to decide whether enough information has been gathered to answer the question originally posed. For example, if differences in shelving productivity are found to be caused by congestion in the aisles in the busier branches (a customer-use pattern), that finding will answer the question "Why are there differences?" If other significant variables aren't uncovered, the study can stop at this point.

Listen carefully to the advisory group's discussion—this will provide important clues to the ways in which other staff will think about the data that's been gathered and the conclusions that are being drawn from it. A story is developing—pay attention to its development and its power. Does it seem true? Do the motivations ring true? Are the actions convincing? Conclusive?

Assistance with Project Implementation

The advisory group can also assist with the actual implementation activities. Group members can be very helpful in generating lists of work activities or tasks to be analyzed. This generation by experts is essential to ensuring that the correct work tasks are identified and that terms are used that will be understandable to others doing the work. However, using the advisory group experts doesn't guarantee agreement, so members can assist in soliciting feedback from others.

Group members might also be asked to keep logs (either personally or through other members of their work unit) or to conduct observations of work tasks. While there are advantages and disadvantages to various data-collection methods, involving members of the advisory group should ensure a higher level of accuracy and validity than doing it without their assistance.

Assistance with Communication throughout the Library

The members of the advisory group can play a crucial role in keeping staff throughout the library informed about the purpose and progress of the workload analysis project. Staff members who might be skeptical about managerial communications are more likely to be responsive to communications from their colleagues and peers. Advisory group members could be involved in developing a librarywide communication plan, in creating question-and-answer documents, and in hosting formal or informal meetings to discuss the project.

Of course, it is critical that all of the advisory group members have the same information and send the same message when they are communicating about the project. That means that a part of each advisory group meeting should probably be devoted to discussing how to inform the rest of the staff about what occurred during the meeting. It can be helpful to prepare a one-page summary of issues discussed and decisions made at each meeting to provide a framework for library-wide communications.

Understanding Project Management

While a full-blown description of project management tools and techniques is outside the scope of this book, a few reminders and references may help you think through the steps of developing your workload analysis project. These are not steps unique to workload analysis; they are the general steps for managing any project you might undertake in your library.

One of the best, most practical books on the topic defines project management this way:

> Project management is the process by which actions are planned, resources organized, and activities initiated and managed to achieve a specific goal or purpose or to produce a specified deliverable.[1]

This definition basically captures the steps in any project planning activity:

- Develop the project goal.
- Identify needed resources and project constraints.
- Identify potential trouble areas or hot spots.
- Break the project down into major and minor subdivisions, and identify the tasks that go with each.
- Sequence the necessary tasks, and develop a tracking methodology.
- Assign responsibility for each part of the project.
- Prioritize and schedule each task.
- Develop the project budget.
- Review the plan, revise it as necessary, and obtain final approval.

The Project Goal

The project goal is a restatement of the purpose for undertaking the workload analysis project. This purpose might be driven by a need to obtain information, such as what is the staffing level needed in the new branch or what are the productivity levels of the clerks in technical services. On the other hand, it might be driven by a perceived problem, such as why is there a shelving backlog in the East Branch when the West Branch, with the same number of staff and the same circulation, doesn't have a backlog.

It is very important that your goal is unambiguous and that it includes a clear statement of what you expect to accomplish. In other words, the goal needs to define what success will look like when the project is complete. Defining success up front will eliminate one of the biggest reasons for project failure: the project's failing to meet expectations. Be sure to identify *whose* expectations are to be met and to communicate this to others involved in the project. If you think the project will be a success if it tells you how you can get more productivity out of a branch team that seems to be underperforming but the branch manager thinks it will be a success if she gets more clerk hours assigned to her branch, the project may well create more problems than it solves.

Feeling comfortable with the project goal is obviously necessary for a successful project. The goal statement should be SMART:

Specific — This will help you define the scope of the project and help ensure that you collect only data that you need.

Measurable — Because this project is about workload analysis, you have to be sure that what you do can be defined and measured.

Achievable — Don't bite off more than you can chew. Do you have the time, expertise, and resources to do it? Kill the project here if an honest answer is "no."

Relevant — Be sure that this project makes sense when you look at everything else: your service priorities, current budget situation, and planning environment. Again, if it fails this test, stop at this point.

Time-dimensioned — A project is different from ongoing work because it has a definite end. If this project is important, it must have a deadline for completion, even if that deadline is general at the planning stage.

Defining success does not mean that the goal statement presupposes a single solution. Project findings and conclusions are usually not susceptible to binary analysis (yes/no or right/wrong) but instead reveal an interrelated network of causes, effects, and influences.

Project Constraints and Possible Hot Spots

The discipline required to follow project management steps comes into focus as you move through the project planning steps. Undertaking the workload analysis project itself requires an assessment of the time it will take to conduct the data gathering and analysis activities and an assessment of the skills needed to successfully implement the project. A crucial part of project planning is understanding the constraints on any project (quality, schedule, and resources) and understanding that it is inevitable that trade-offs will have to be made during the project. By asking questions about your priorities as you begin, you will be better prepared to address the variances that arise. If it appears that your time frame can't be met, can you add more people to the project? If misunderstandings arise about the data collection methodology and you get lower quality data than you wanted, can you live with it, or do you need to collect data again?

Identifying potential hot spots or trouble areas in advance will also help ensure the project's success. Brainstorming and mind mapping are two effective idea-generation techniques that can produce a large number of ideas in a nonthreatening context. Brainstorming involves asking a group to respond to a question, issue, or problem with as many ideas as they can in a relatively short, 5- to 20-minute period of time. As the ideas are generated, they are recorded and clarified but not judged or debated. People can either spontaneously call the ideas out or provide them in go-around-the-room fashion. Because a number of people are focusing on the issue together, many more ideas can be generated, much faster, than using other techniques. People's ideas are stimulated as they see the ideas of others, and the absence of judgment encourages a looser, more creative thought process.

Mind mapping is another technique that encourages the free-flowing generation of ideas. It also results in an overall picture of the project, problem, or issue. Because it involves drawing and picturing ideas in a nonlinear way, it can stimulate a different kind of thinking and creativity than simply working with words or a conventional outline.[2]

Mind mapping can be done on an individual basis or as a group activity. Begin by placing the central idea, concept, or question in the middle of the paper. (See figure 3.) Draw branches from this central point as related ideas or concepts occur. One branch can lead to another in a web or network of ideas and thoughts. Unrelated ideas can appear as additional branches. Use pictures, colors, and symbols to amplify and illustrate the thinking as it bursts forward. Because ideas radiate out from the central point, you can jump from point to point in a way that linear outlining doesn't easily allow. You'll be surprised at both the number of ideas that spring forth and the complexity that you're able to capture on one sheet of paper.

If the advisory group is used to generate ideas, an added benefit will be to get concerns out in the open at the beginning of the project and to begin the process, as a group, of working either to answer the concerns or to come up with ways to resolve them. Again, if a problem

FIGURE 3
Mind Map

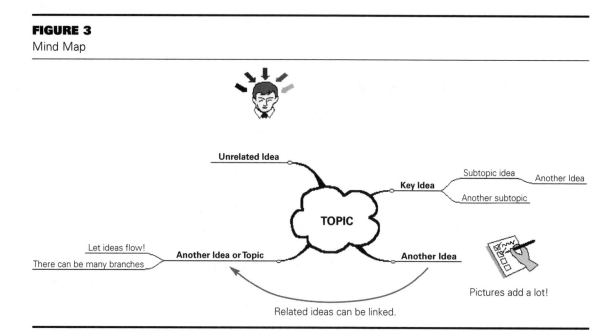

is identified that makes the project impossible to pursue, it is better to find out at the beginning rather than waste time and resources and fail along the way.

CASE STUDY

TREE COUNTY PUBLIC LIBRARY REFERENCE SERVICES

Zeke meets with the two librarians and the library assistant who volunteered for the project advisory group. He provides them with an outline to follow so they know what they need to discuss and plan. They talk about what they are trying to learn and decide that the statistics they currently keep reflect only part of what they do. Everyone starts talking at once, so Zeke starts writing down all the ideas they have about what staff does at the reference desk. The volume increases when someone mentions the problems they have to deal with such as unruly library users, people actually fighting over the PCs, and all the calls that came into the desk about tax forms. Zeke reminds them that they are just listing ideas at this point, and he works to catch up with all the words flying around him.

"Well," he says, "it looks like we really need to figure out how people spend their time . . . and how long each sort of thing takes." He suggests that they gather information about exactly what work is done at the reference desk, by whom, and how long it takes. He asks the committee if they feel they can gather this information within the next couple of months, in time for him to have the information for his budget submission. They think it can be done.

At this point, Myra says, "How are we going to do this? I think people are going to freak out if we show up with clipboards and stopwatches. You know some people already think this is all about replacing us with more computers or something. And if you want this done for the budget, does that mean we're finally going to get more people?"

Zeke gulps. These must be the hot spots he'd read about.

As you can see, a workload analysis project can generate a myriad of issues and concerns you might want to investigate. Focusing on the goal is a crucial element of planning.

Project Outline and Sequence

One approach to project planning suggests that the planner divide the project up into large hunks, smaller chunks, and even smaller bites.[3] This division process works even better if more than one person is involved—another area where the advisory group can assist.

"Large hunks" are the major subdivisions of the project. In a workload analysis project, they might include project definition, information gathering, data analysis, and the communication plan. "Chunks" are the next pieces—subdivisions of the hunks. Information gathering, for example, could include workform selection, location and/or work unit selection, and data collection. The "bites," then, are the actions necessary to make the project happen. Under workform selection, for example, the project manager and advisory group would meet, discuss the workforms available, and select those that are to be used. Another bite would be to devise the data collection schedule and distribute it. Bites are the kinds of activities that can be assigned to someone to do and that can be tracked to ensure completion.

A number of techniques can be used to plan the project. Some people use an outline approach as shown in figure 4. Others like to draw diagrams, use flowcharts as shown in figure 5, or use sticky notes that can be moved around until the major divisions and steps in the process are clear. As you plan, you may find yourself going back to add steps or tasks you missed the first time through, so choose a technique that

---

FIGURE 4
Project Outline

I. Project Definition
    A. Develop project goal/problem statement
    B. Appoint project team
        1. Select project manager
        2. Select advisory group
            a. Hold first meeting to present process and advisory group role
    C. Select type of analysis: numeric or process?
II. Information Gathering
    A. Select location/work units to study
    B. Select workforms to use
        1. Conduct pretests to develop controlled vocabulary
    C. Assess existing data for usefulness
    D. Collect additional data as needed
        1. Develop and distribute data collection schedule
        2. Train staff to complete workforms
        3. Appoint line staff to distribute and collect workforms in each work unit
III. Data Analysis
    A. Review workforms
        1. Used standard vocabulary?
        2. Collected and reported data per instructions?
    B. Perform calculations
    C. Assess results for validity and applicability to problem statement
        1. Determine appropriate analysis technique for data
        2. Determine best method for presenting results
IV. Communication Plan
    A. Announce project plans
        1. Determine who needs to know
        2. Select multiple appropriate means of communication
    B. Deliver ongoing status reports
        1. Determine who needs to know
        2. Select multiple appropriate means of communication
    C. Release project results/findings
        1. Determine who needs to know
        2. Select multiple appropriate means of communication

---

FIGURE 5
Project Flowchart

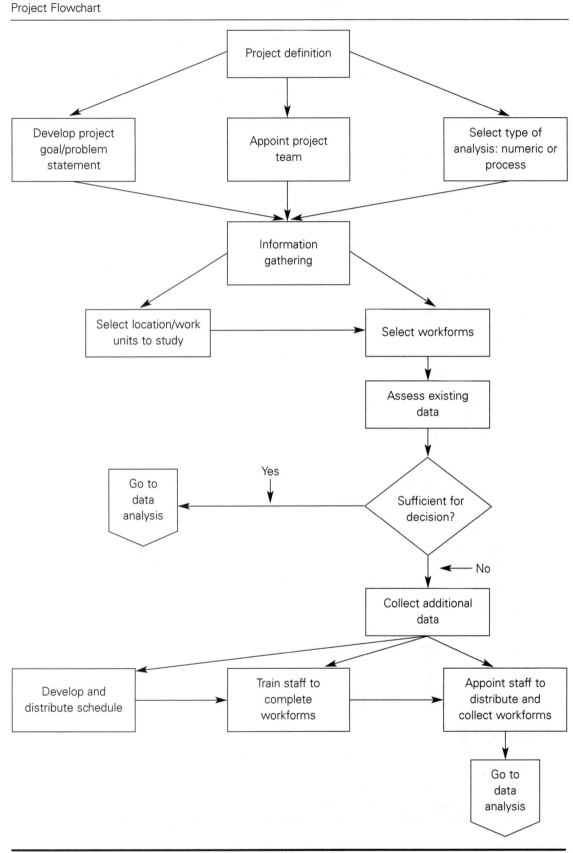

is easy to edit. Whichever method you employ, use verbs to identify each step, since these are *actions* that someone will take.

Once it appears that the major pieces and tasks have been identified, sequence the tasks so that it's clear what has to be done before something else can be done, which tasks are dependent upon other tasks, which tasks can be carried out at the same time, and so on. Then enter these sequenced tasks on planning workforms or finalize them in a project management computer program. In a workload analysis project, for example, the workforms have to be selected before they can be distributed. Obviously, the data can't be analyzed until the workforms are completed and sent in, and the meeting or time to review the data depends upon those who gather the information meeting their schedule.

Project Responsibilities and Budget

After the tasks are known and put in order, assign responsibility so that the tasks are carried out. Also assign dates for completion at this point. Write down these assignments so that everyone knows what is to be done, who is going to do it, and what the deadlines are. This is vital information for the project and for communicating to the rest of the staff, so they understand the project and know who's going to be involved and what the time line is.

This is a good time to make another resource assessment. Will the people assigned be able to meet their assignments as well as carry out their other assigned tasks in the library? Is one name appearing so often that it looks like that person will be overwhelmed? Are the time lines realistic in light of other activities, holidays, vacations, and other commitments?

Once all of the steps and players have been identified and the time line has been established, the budget can be prepared. Depending upon the design and complexity of the project, you may want to compute staff costs, costs for replacement staff if staff who are working on the project will be replaced by others, costs for any necessary equipment, computer processing time, costs for professional services, costs for reproduction of workforms and manuals, etc.

Project Approval

The final step in the project planning process is to secure final approval of the project, the basic approach, and the estimated cost. If the director initiated the project, the approval may come from the library board or city or county manager. If a project manager has been appointed, the director should see and agree to the project plan before proceeding. This is the time to lay everything out, make any necessary revisions, and ask one more time if the project is viable. Will the resources be available? Is the time line realistic within the context of everything else the library is doing? What tradeoffs will be acceptable if problems are encountered along the way?

Defining Your Workload Analysis Project

The project management steps presented in the previous sections could apply to most projects in the library. However, every project has its own unique characteristics as well. If you are going to apply for a grant, you need to know the financial limitations of the grantor before you start planning. You would probably design a very different project if the top limit were $10,000 than you would if you knew the top limit were $100,000. Before you can actually design your workload analysis project you have to decide what it is you want to measure and analyze and how much detail you think you will need to make informed decisions.

Approaches to Workload Analysis

Once you define the outcomes of your workload analysis project, you will be in a position to decide which approach will provide you with the data you need to accomplish those outcomes. The two most common reasons for undertaking a workload analysis project are to assess the performance of your organization or to solve a problem. Begin by deciding which you are trying to do.

Performance assessment or performance monitoring (these terms are used interchangeably) is done through *numeric analysis.* This requires establishing a *baseline* measurement and then comparing ongoing results with that baseline.

Problem solving usually involves *process analysis,* understanding how work is done in your organization.

Using numeric measures to monitor performance involves calculating workloads from statistical information. Information on the amount of staff time spent, also called *effort,* and number of measurable results produced, or *outputs,* can be used to determine numeric measures. Because you start with numbers, your results are numeric, for example, number of hours spent assisting the public with technology or number of items weeded per staff hour. Performance monitoring done with numeric values is done through a *longitudinal study.* This means that you compare several sets of data collected over time to determine if there were any significant changes in the numbers. Progressively increasing or decreasing numbers represent a *trend,* a nonrandom change in the results. Trends can signal developing problems or confirm performance improvements.

Process analysis is a key component of problem solving through studying workloads. It involves analyzing the steps in a task. The outcomes of process analysis might include identifying ways to make the work easier to perform, increasing the productivity of the staff members performing the work, or reducing the costs of the task. Process analysis is done by identifying the steps in a task, questioning the need for each step, and searching for ways to improve those steps that are necessary.

Numeric analysis and process analysis may be used separately or together. If you are monitoring the performance of activities you believe to be efficient and effective, numeric analysis alone may be sufficient for your purposes. If you believe that some tasks in an activity are unnecessary or that some steps in a task may be unnecessary, then analyzing the tasks, questioning what you find, and eliminating or redesigning steps may be enough to achieve your objectives.

Sometimes the results of numeric analysis will prompt you to conduct a process analysis to search for explanations for a trend you have discovered. After you change the steps in a task, you may want to set up a data collection routine that will allow you to monitor your results through periodic numeric analysis. Both of these tools are valuable in a variety of situations, and you'll want to know how to use each one for your workload analyses.

There is also the question of detail. Workload analysis can range from very general to very detailed analyses. It is often an iterative process in which each set of data you develop suggests additional areas you could study. It is easy to be distracted by interesting results that lead you to ask "I wonder why . . . ?" You can find yourself in an endless data collection mode that never results in any changes in your library's operations. A clear statement of your objective, such as "monitor the number of items processed per staff hour worked" or "identify the number of steps to approve a payment" will help you know when you have achieved your objective for this analysis. When you learn what you need to know, stop studying, make a decision, and move on. Don't let yourself get seduced by the lure of collecting more data than you need or wandering down interesting paths that are not relevant to your objective. This doesn't mean that you never follow up on other things you discover; it just means that you should begin at the beginning, with a clear statement of your objective, before you start collecting another set of data.

Workload Analysis Activities

The activities in a workload analysis project are the same whether you are doing a numeric analysis or a process analysis.

1. Begin by defining what you want to accomplish. Establish your objective and determine what criteria you will use to know when you

have achieved that objective. What will success look like at the end of this project? Which of the two types of analysis—numeric or process—are you undertaking?

2. Identify what you need to know. What are the factors that affect your goal?

3. Determine if you are presently collecting some or all of the data you need. Is this an old problem or a new problem? If it is an old problem, you may already have considerable data about it.

4. Ask if the data you already have provides an answer. If it does, stop here, make a decision, and move on to other things.

5. Determine what additional data you need if you do not already have enough to make a decision. Do you need to know who does the work? How it is done? How long the task or steps take? How many outputs are produced? Does the data need to be precise, or will estimates do?

6. Decide how you will gather the data. This book and the included workforms are intended to help you with this task.

7. Analyze the new data to determine if it gives you enough information to accomplish your objective. If it does, make your decision.

8. Ask yourself if any additional information would cause you to change your mind about the decision you are making or would provide the additional information needed to make a decision. If the answer is no, you are done. If the answer is yes, then you may need to delve deeper by returning to step 1 to establish a new objective and collect more detailed information or perform more complex calculations. This is the iterative part of workload analysis, but you should only pursue it if further information might lead you to a different decision.

Workform 1, Workload Analysis Project Overview, will help you organize the project. It provides a place to record the project goal, to identify the data, and to define how you will know when you have enough information to make a decision.

Chapter 3 provides the methods and tools you need to use basic numeric analysis, and chapter 4 describes the methods and tools you need to complete a basic process analysis. Chapter 5 provides more in-depth tools and analysis techniques to be used if you find that you still have unanswered questions after using the basic methods.

How Precise Do You Need to Be?

Before you embark on any workload analysis project, clearly identify who will use the data and for what purpose. Collect only what you need to know to support the identified purpose. The level of precision needed for workload analysis is linked to the intended user and use of the information. If a library director is trying to determine whether circulation staff is appropriately distributed across multiple agencies, it may be sufficient to measure circulation per staff hour in each agency. However, if unexplained variances are found, the heads of circulation in those agencies may need more detailed data on the number of library cards issued, the number of holds placed, etc., and the amount of time required by each of these component tasks so you can answer questions about why significant variations exist among their agencies.

The first rule of data collection is to collect only that data you plan to use for a specific end. Collecting data can be time-consuming and expensive. If you cannot or will not make changes based on the information you develop, don't spend time and money developing it. The corollary to this is to collect only data you will use soon. Conditions in the library are changing too rapidly to act on old data.

The greater the level of detail or accuracy that you require to make your decisions, the more effort you will have to put into the data collection and the more expensive that data becomes. Remember, too, that while the existing statistics or data you have may appear on the surface to be accurate, they probably aren't as accurate as you think. In many public libraries statistics are kept with varying levels of control over consistency of definition and data collection procedures.

Most library managers are familiar with the problems and confusions that can arise when more than one staff member is involved in collecting data about the same task. Just think about the process used in your library to count the number of reference questions asked. You probably use a hash-mark system—most libraries do. That often means that busy staff members stop after a rush of work and say, "We certainly have been busy; I'll bet we had a dozen questions in the last 30 minutes" and so someone makes 12 hash marks on the tally form. This may or may not be an informed guess, but it is certainly not an absolutely accurate count.

The output statistics produced by an automated system are probably the most accurate data you have. However, if you use system-generated statistics, you should be sure that you know what the statistic is counting before you make decisions based on the data. Different systems use different terminology, and statistics that you think measure one thing may well measure something else. For example, some systems may count as a renewal any item that was not listed as "on shelf" at the time of the charge, while others may count only those transactions completed in the process of renewal.

A lot of the statistics that you collect are required by your state library agency, which is in turn required to submit them to the National Center for Education Statistics (NCES). This requirement is based on the School Improvement Act of 1988 (PL 100-297). That law gives NCES broad powers *"to acquire and diffuse among the people of the U.S. useful statistical information on subjects connected with education* (in the most general and comprehensive sense of the word). Libraries are identified as one of those 'subjects.' In addition, the law states: the Center [NCES] with the assistance of the State library agencies *shall develop and support a cooperative system of annual data collection for public libraries.*[4] While the data you report provides valuable information for state and national planning purposes, much of it is too general to be useful in a workload analysis project.

Other data you currently collect also may be too general for the level of precision you need. For example, you know the number of hours a week of circulation clerk time you have budgeted, and that may be sufficient to determine the average number of circulation transactions per FTE (full-time equivalent) staff. However, if you are trying to decide how to allocate a limited number of circulation staff across several units, you will probably need more precise data. You may need the number of budgeted full-time and part-time employee hours as well as temporary or substitute hours. The actual usage of clerk hours could vary from branch to branch even though the budgeted number of hours is the same.

Remember, too, that FTE staff numbers don't really represent 2,080 hours of effort each year. Vacations, holidays, even daily breaks can reduce the actual hours worked significantly. The workform developed for *Managing for Results* to calculate actual hours available has been reproduced in this book as Workform 2, Estimate of Productive Work Hours Available. You can use it to develop more precise work-hour data for your library if general staffing estimates won't do. A completed example of Workform 2 is shown in figure 6.

It is important to realize that very little, if any, of the data you have historically kept is absolutely accurate. Achieving a level of unimpeachable accuracy in data collection is far too expensive for most organizations, and it is not really necessary to make good decisions. Start your data-collection efforts at a "big picture" level, especially if this is your first experience with workload analysis. You can always delve deeper later if you find you want or need more detail or precision.

NOTES

1. Jeff Crow, *Applying Project Management in the Workplace* (Portland, Ore.: Blackbird, 1999), 1–2.

2. Mindmapping was developed by Tony Buzan, who has written several books about the technique. A more accessible introduction, however, is provided by Joyce Wycoff, *Mindmapping: Your Personal Guide to Exploring Creativity and Problem-Solving* (New York: Berkley, 1991).

3. G. Lynne Snead and Joyce Wycoff, *To Do . . . Doing . . . Done!* (New York: Simon & Schuster, 1997), 145–51.

4. Purpose of FSCS [National Center for Education Statistics]. Available www.nclis.gov/libraries/lsp/purpose.html. 9 Sept. 2001.

FIGURE 6

Completed Example of Workform 2: Estimate of Productive Work Hours Available

A. Indicate the number and level of staff in **one** of the categories below.

Librarians _____ Library assistants __8__ Clerical _____ Pages _____

B. Unit/team ___Ash Branch___

C. Number of staff eligible for benefits __8__ for standard vacation __6__ for seniority vacation __2__

D. Hours in standard work week __40__

E. Nominal staff hours available per year: number of staff __8__ × hours in standard work week __40__ × 52 weeks/yr. = __16,640__

F. Nominal staff hours available/year			16,640
G. Predictable hours unavailable			
1. Vacation			
Standard vacation hours [80 at Ash] × number of staff eligible [6]	480		
Seniority vacation hours [80 at Ash] × number of staff eligible [2]	160		
2. Holidays (in hours)	640		
3. Daily customary breaks (2 × 15 min. × number staff)	960		
4. Other	0		
5. Total predictable hours unavailable		2,240	
H. Unpredictable hours unavailable			
1. Sick leave	192		
2. Personal days	128		
3. Other	40		
4. Total unpredictable hours unavailable		360	
I. Grand total hours unavailable			−2,600
J. Actual full-time staff hours available for year			14,040
K. Number hours of part-time staff budgeted this year			+1,000
L. Total hours available for this level per year			15,040

41

Chapter 3

Basic Numeric Analysis

MILESTONES

By the time you finish this chapter you will know how to

- assess existing numeric data for its relevance to your project goals

- develop data on the level of effort used to create an output

- create a standard vocabulary that supports data gathering in multiple work units or at different points in time

- determine which data gathering technique best meets the needs of the project

- develop and use baseline measurements

Numeric analysis is the process of measuring the outputs produced with a particular amount of effort and developing numeric standards that will allow you to monitor performance on an ongoing basis through periodic measurement and statistical analysis. Numeric analysis requires that you establish a baseline measurement and then compare ongoing results with that baseline.

You can certainly compute numeric measures for any activity in the library, but you will probably want to start with an analysis of an activity that will provide the most bang for the buck. That suggests that you start with a fairly broad scope when you identify the purpose of your workload measure project and define the goal of the project. A broad project goal will allow you to look at an area in which you expend substantial staff resources and about which you may well have output data that can be linked with this expenditure of staff time.

Using Existing Output Data

All libraries keep some measures of output (items checked out, items processed, reference questions answered, etc.) and effort (staff hours) that can be used to develop general numeric measures. Let's look at how the Tree County Public Library's technical services supervisor uses current statistics to develop numeric measures of her department's work.

CASE STUDY

TREE COUNTY PUBLIC LIBRARY TECHNICAL SERVICES

Remember that you learned in chapter 1 about Tree County Public Library's plans to spend $50,000 on nonprint materials in the new fiscal year? The director kept her commitment and provided an additional 20 hours a week of staffing to handle the increased workload.

The technical services department head, Bev Bingham, used those 20 hours to increase both the cataloging hours and the processing hours in the department. Since she has 2.5 FTE catalogers and only 1 FTE processing staff member who also handles the mail (approximately a 3:1 ratio), Bev put 15 hours into cataloging and 5 hours into processing (another intuitive decision). The push to provide more nonprint materials is a key goal of the library, so Bev told her staff to catalog and process nonprint materials first.

At the end of the first month, there was a backlog of print materials totaling nearly 200 titles. By the end of the third month, public services staff was beginning to complain about how long it took to receive print materials. Bev told the catalogers to handle two trucks of new print materials for every one truck of nonprint to balance the flow of materials through the department. The backlog continued to grow.

Bev studied the statistics from the previous year and projections for this year:

	This Year	Last Year
Print titles added	22,500	22,500
Nonprint titles added	5,000	2,500
Annual total	27,500	25,000
Weekly hours of available cataloger time	115 per week	100 per week
Weekly cataloging workload (Annual total divided by weekly hours)	239	250

The workloads are actually less for the catalogers this year than last, but the backlog is growing. Now what?

For most library work the output measures and the effort data are not so easily linked. Developing basic numeric measures often requires combining the available data in new ways or separating an output or effort measure into its component parts to make it more usable.

As noted in chapter 2, the first steps in any workload analysis project are to decide what work you want to study, define the purpose of the project, and identify who will use the results you create. Based on those decisions, you will determine your approach to workload analysis: numeric analysis or process analysis. If you decide that numeric analysis is the appropriate approach, your next step will be to consider what data you will need to achieve your purpose.

Begin by reviewing the areas in which you already collect output data to see if you are already collecting some of the data you will need. Every library keeps a variety of statistical data to track the number of services delivered, the number of users served, or the number of hours of service offered. These existing statistics may be useful in developing basic numeric measures. In the preceding example, Bev had existing statistics that enabled her to calculate the cataloging workload.

Consider the actual activities and tasks you are presently measuring in your library as sources of data for computing numeric measures. Every library will have a slightly different combination of data available, but most libraries will have something. None of these statistics by themselves are numeric workload measures, but many of these statistics can be combined with staffing data and used to calculate numeric measures.

For instance, if you are interested in comparing the workload of circulation clerks in seven branches, you could look at the circulation for the period you're interested in and divide it by the number of hours of circulation clerk time assigned to the branches. The Tree County Public Library gathered such data, presented in figure 7.

Is this a totally accurate picture of the relative circulation workloads in the Tree County Public Library branches? No. We know that circulation clerks probably do other things besides check library materials in

FIGURE 7
Existing Data Example

Branch	FY Circulation	Number of FTE Circulation Clerks	Annual Circulation per FTE
Ash	113,396	4.0	28,349
Birch	104,461	3.5	29,846
Elm	176,780	4.0	44,195
Fir	112,848	4.0	28,212
Maple	330,464	8.0	41,308
Oak	203,472	5.5	36,995
Pine	100,797	3.5	28,799

and out. The likelihood is high, however, that the mix of work among the circulation clerks in these seven branches is similar enough that this analysis will at least provide a first level of information.

Despite the imprecise nature of much of your current data, using it to develop numeric measures will give you much more information than you had before. The very activity of gathering information about effort and looking at it in conjunction with output data to derive numeric measurements will cause you to be more aware of how you use staff resources than you have ever been before. You will be asking yourself questions such as "Am I getting the whole picture?" "Am I evaluating this information before me fairly?" "What else do I need to know?"

Establishing Baseline Measurements

The first time you measure anything you are establishing a starting point for future measurements. This starting point, or baseline measurement, brings meaning to your measures by providing a comparison point. If you know that last month technical services staff processed 15 new books an hour, is that a reasonable rate of output? Without a baseline you can't make judgments about numeric measures. If you knew that the month before the technical services output was 10 new books an hour, then you would be pleased at the improvement. If the previous month's output was 25 an hour, you would be concerned about the drop in productivity. Without a baseline it is hard to interpret the meaning of a measurement.

Developing Data on Effort

The key to using existing data for basic numeric measures is that there must be a clear link between the staff hours worked and output produced. For example, in the Bark County Public Library circulation clerks work only at the circulation desk. Therefore, there is a clear connection between the hours circulation clerks worked and the annual circulation of materials. Calculating the circulation staff workload will be a fairly straightforward matter of dividing output by effort to arrive at workload. To come up with a numeric measure, divide the output measurement by the effort that it took to produce that work. For example:

$$\frac{8{,}465 \text{ circulations per week (output)}}{200 \text{ clerical staff hours per week (effort)}} = \frac{42 \text{ circulations per}}{\text{staff hour (workload)}}$$

However, in the Tree County Public Library, circulation clerks and paraprofessionals who work in circulation also share information desk responsibilities. Calculating the circulation staff workload will be a more complex process in this environment.

Who Does What and When?

In many areas of library work, using existing staffing data can be difficult. You may have a statistic for the number of new titles cataloged each month and information on the number of people assigned to the technical services department. However, in this case you can't just divide the number of titles cataloged by the number of staff to determine the staff workload because many of the staff in technical services do tasks that are not directly linked to cataloging new books. You may know the number of librarians on staff who select materials and the number of titles purchased each year. Again, you can't determine the staff workload by dividing the number of titles purchased by the number of staff who select materials because the librarians do more than just select titles; they also answer reference questions, do story hours, plan programs, etc.

If you can't identify a clear link between an output and the staff that produce the output, how can you establish a numeric measure? First you must decide why there isn't a clear link between the output and your staffing information. Are you not sure which staff or job classifications contribute to the output? Could one set of outputs be produced by staff in different job classifications in each of your work units? If you are unsure about who actually does the work you want to measure, Workform 3, Determining Who Does What, will help you identify which staff or job classifications are responsible for the outputs.

One challenge when completing a form like Workform 3 is that there are often multiple people who actually perform a task in a work unit with a small staff. Although circulation may be primarily the responsibility of the clerical staff, in a small branch the librarian may fill in there during breaks or help out when people are waiting in line. Everyone in technical services may pitch in to unpack new books when a large shipment arrives. In these instances, the first step is to determine the primary and secondary responsibilities of the staff involved. Workform 3 provides a way to report both of these levels of responsibility by asking the person completing the workform to identify his or her primary and secondary responsibilities.

Before you ask staff to complete Workform 3, you need to think through the level of detail and precision that will accomplish the goal of your workload analysis project. Workform 3 is meant to help you develop a general overall picture of who does what work in a unit or facility. Theoretically, many if not all staff members may do virtually anything and everything, especially in an emergency or crunch situation. When filling out the form, encourage staff to attempt to describe the normal work and backup assignments, not all the possible contingency arrangements that could arise.

In the Workform 3 example shown in figure 8, *P* indicates that staff in this job class have primary responsibility for the task and *S* indicates that they have secondary or backup responsibilities for the task. Although this data is fairly general, it can be surprisingly informative. You will not only get a more accurate picture of the responsibilities in each work unit, you may well discover some inefficient use of staff that you could easily correct.

Use a Standard Vocabulary

In figure 8, column C lists the tasks being studied. If you have more than one work unit to be studied or more than one person who is responsible for performing the activities or tasks you are studying, it is crucial that consistent terms be used to describe the activities or tasks. Without consistency of terms you cannot compare data among staff or work units.

The importance of a standard vocabulary when describing a task can't be overemphasized. Think about the problem you would have if you were trying to determine numeric measures pertaining to circulation, and staff in one branch included shelving as a part of the circulation function while staff in another branch considered shelving as a separate task. Clearly, the data you collect from the two branches will not be comparable. It would probably appear that the circulation staff in the second branch were much more efficient than the staff in the first branch when, if you had used a standard definition for "circulation," you might well have found that their workloads were similar.

If your numeric measures project is focused on measures at the task level, you will want to involve the staff who perform those tasks in the process of defining the terms to be used to describe the tasks. *Pretesting* is a way to develop terms and definitions that will be understandable and

FIGURE 8
Completed Example of Workform 3: Determining Who Does What

A. Location and/or work unit   Oak Branch

B. Activity   Reference services

C. **Tasks**	**D. Job Classification or Name:** Librarian I	**D. Job Classification or Name:** Library Assistant	**D. Job Classification or Name:** Library Clerk	**D. Job Classification or Name:**
1. Staffing the information desk	P	P		
2. Selecting materials	P			
3. Holds processing		S	P	
4.				
5.				
6.				
7.				
8.				
9.				
10.				
11.				
12.				
13.				
14.				
15.				

recognizable to your staff. You can use Workform 3 as a way to pretest terms and definitions for tasks. Workform 4, Standard Terms in Our Library for Tasks and Steps, can be used to record and distribute the agreed-upon definitions. Figure 9 is an example of a completed Workform 4.

To pretest for terms to use in studying tasks:

1. Distribute Workform 3 to a representative group of staff in the work units being studied. Ask them to complete the workforms individually.

2. Collect and review the completed workforms looking for common terms for tasks in these work units. This can be done either by a single person or in a group composed of staff that completed the workforms.

3. Select or develop one term for each task from among those submitted and write the term and its definition on Workform 4, Standard Terms in Our Library for Tasks and Steps.

4. Collect all of the relevant Workform 4s that describe the activities and tasks in the work units you are studying and distribute them with Workform 3. Tell staff to use *only* these terms for recording tasks in the workforms they complete. Impress upon staff that these are the only terms to be used, explaining that otherwise you will have problems comparing sets of data.

There is another standardization issue to consider as well. If you plan to do a *longitudinal study,* comparing workloads over time, each time the data is collected it must represent the same steps in the same tasks to be validly comparable. If your data gathering focuses on a specific task done in more than one work unit or by more than one staff member, you'll need to control the vocabulary that describes the steps in the task, just as you controlled the vocabulary for the tasks themselves. Chapter 4 contains information about how to determine the steps within a task, including information on developing a common vocabulary to describe the steps in tasks.

Describing Public Desk Work

Many staff and even some managers believe that it is impossible to quantify the work performed at public desks, particularly reference desks. The argument is made that there are so many different types of work done at public desks that it is impossible to describe them all or to clearly identify when one type of task stops and another begins. This is only true if you try to capture data on every aspect of what happens at the desk.

It may not be practical to try to distinguish between the time spent answering reference questions and the time spent answering directional questions, but it is possible to distinguish between direct patron

FIGURE 9

Completed Example of Workform 4: Standard Terms in Our Library for Tasks and Steps

A. Activity: Providing services at the information desk

B. Description: This activity includes answering reference and directional questions, searching for requested titles
and placing holds, collection management, and reader's advisory work.

C. Task: _____

D. (Tasks/Steps)	E. Definition
1. Holds	Includes searching shelves for materials and placing holds for materials not found
2. Information service	Includes answering directional and reference questions and providing instruction on the OPAC and electronic databases
3. Collection management	Includes reading reviews, ordering materials, weeding the collection, and changing shelving locations in the OPAC as needed
4. Reader's advisory	Includes providing advice on reading selections
5.	
6.	
7.	
8.	

service and tasks performed during the "wait" periods when there are no patrons at the desk or when the phone isn't ringing.

In the simplest set of descriptions, you can distinguish between direct patron service and other work. Likewise, if there is a particular component of desk work you are interested in studying, the tasks associated with that work could be grouped together under a single term that describes a collection of tasks. For example, rather than describe the range of tasks associated with public PCs as "show patrons how to use computer," "fix printer problems," and "help patron search licensed database," you could aggregate all of these tasks under the single term of "PC assistance."

Zeke and the reference work advisory group decide to use their brainstorm list of reference work as the beginning point for completing Workform 4: Standard Terms in Our Library for Tasks and Steps. After discussion they aggregate items on their list into five tasks:

answer patron questions (informational and directional)

provide readers' assistance

assist patrons with using catalog and other electronic reference sources

assist patrons with using PCs (sign-ups and problems with using equipment)

deal with unruly patrons/security issues

Agreeing on these tasks and definitions is hard, and group members have trouble keeping their focus on the project goal "to figure out how people spend their time . . . and how long each sort of thing takes."

Group members feel they are identifying what needs to be studied. They ask Zeke what's already known about the reference desk workload. He answers that he has statistics on reference questions, which is why he knows that they've fallen off 20 percent over the last two years even though nothing unusual has happened: The hours are the same, and staffing has remained the same.

"Yeah," interjects Don, "but now nearly 50 percent of the county has Internet access. People are obviously finding answers to their own questions!"

"Not at my branch," retorts Susan. "The folks who use Birch can barely feed their families. They can't afford to buy a computer or pay the monthly fees for Internet access. That's why all those kids come in after school."

Zeke tells the group that reference statistics, while gathered from each branch, are always presented as a systemwide total. He hasn't really looked that closely at differences among the branches or at how trends might differ among the branches.

After you develop a standard vocabulary to define tasks, you often discover that your current statistics measure some, but not all, of the tasks. Even those that are measured may not be recorded in ways that are useful for your workload analysis.

Establishing the Link between Effort and Output

Even after you know who does the work you are studying and you are confident that the terms being used are comparable, you may still have a problem establishing a link between effort and output because the staff that produce the output also do other things with their time. If so, you will need to collect more data to determine what portion of each staff member's or job classification's time is spent on the output you want to use.

There are three ways to obtain the information you need:

- estimates
- self-reports
- observations

Estimates

Many numeric analysis projects begin with asking people to estimate the amount of time they spend on various tasks. The information obtained from this method will only be as reliable as the estimating capacity of the person doing it. Some people have a very good sense of how they spend their time and an equally good sense of proportion. It isn't hard for them to think in terms of percentages of time or hours a week they might do something. For others, this is a very difficult exercise. They have a hard time thinking in terms of percentages of time spent on tasks and are flummoxed about how to handle those tasks that come up only occasionally.

The process of estimating time can be complicated by the fact that some people may not trust the motives of the whole data-gathering process. They may either willfully falsify information reported for that reason or because they are afraid that something they think is important will be changed if they don't show that they spend a considerable amount of time doing it. On the other hand, the employees who are asked to estimate the amount of time they spend doing various tasks may feel more positively about this method of gathering data than they do about other methods because they are asked to be involved and because their input is valued as the people closest to the work being studied.

There are two approaches that can be used to estimate the percentages of time staff spend on various tasks or activities. You can ask a unit supervisor to do the estimating for all of the personnel in the unit, or you can ask the individual staff members to do their own estimates. A combination of both of these approaches can provide an effective way to check the validity of the perceptions of the people doing the estimates.

Managers or supervisors will use Workform 5, Estimates of Staff Time: Work Unit Estimate of Time Spent on Activities, to estimate the percentage of staff time that is spent on each assigned task, as shown in figure 10. Workform 6, Estimates of Staff Time: Individual Estimate of Time Spent on Activities, shown in figure 11, can be used by individual staff members to develop time estimates. The estimated percentages can be converted to hours of effort for use in calculating a workload measure.

Clearly, estimating percentages as Workforms 5 and 6 suggest is inexact. However, estimating does have its place because it takes less time and causes less disruption than asking staff to record their activities over a period of time. Furthermore, estimations are often sufficient for the numeric measurements you are trying to develop. If you are interested in very general comparisons of work across multiple agencies or want to compare workloads and performance for a single unit over several time periods, establishing baselines with existing statistics and estimates probably will meet your needs.

Self-Reports

Self-reporting involves asking people to use a standard form to record the tasks they perform during a span of time. Staff may also be asked to record the amount of time needed to perform each task. Workform 7, Recording Staff Tasks: Self-Report Log, provides a form and instructions for gathering self-reported data. A completed example is shown in figure 12.

Self-reporting has the potential advantage of providing more accurate information than the data gathered by estimating. If staff members who are collecting their own data understand the purpose of the workload analysis project, and if their concern about the additional workload caused by having to keep track of activities is acknowledged, self-reports can be effective means of acquiring information.

There are, of course, potential disadvantages to self-reporting. Workers may feel burdened by the data-gathering activity. If they don't understand the purpose of the workload analysis project, they may feel that the whole exercise is pointless or designed to punish underachievers and to make changes in what they are doing. An additional problem is that a personal time log or journal is only as accurate as the person keeping it. A person who is busy may forget to make an entry or try to estimate what she did over a longer period of time than the log calls for. Unless training has been thorough, she may not use terms in a consistent manner or may not keep the journal or log as instructed. Any of these errors could result in entries that are either misleading or useless.

Observation

Observation involves a third party who watches staff perform their duties and records at regular intervals the tasks being performed. Observation can be done either covertly (unobtrusively) or overtly (obtrusively) with the workers aware that they are being observed. Workform 8,

FIGURE 10

Completed Example of Workform 5: Analysis of Staff Time: Work Unit Estimate of Time Spent on Activities

A. Location and/or work unit: _____ Fir Branch _____

B. Activities	C. Job Classification: Librarian I		C. Job Classification: Library Assistant		C. Job Classification: Library Clerk	
	D. % of Full-Time Staff	D. % of Part-Time Staff	D. % of Full-Time Staff	D. % of Part-Time Staff	D. % of Full-Time Staff	D. % of Part-Time Staff
1. Reference services	50%	100%	70%	100%	0%	0%
2. Collection Development	25%	0%	0%	0%	0%	0%
3. Circulation	0%	0%	20%	0%	95%	100%
4. Meetings and other activities	25%		10%		5%	0%
5.						
6.						
7.						
8.						
9.						
10.						
11.						
12.						
13.						
E. Totals	100%	100%	100%	100%	100%	100%

FIGURE 11

Completed Example of Workform 6: Analysis of Staff Time: Individual Estimate
of Time Spent on Activities

A. Location and/or work unit: ___Elm Branch___

B. Job classification: ___Library page___   ☐ FT   ☒ PT

C. Period of time: ☒ daily   ☐ weekly   ☐ monthly

D. Activities	E. % of Time Spent
1. shelving	50%
2. preparing shipment	20%
3. sorting and delivering mail	5%
4. shelf reading	25%
5.	
6.	
7.	
8.	
9.	
10.	
11.	
12.	
13.	
14.	
15.	
F. Total	100%

FIGURE 12

Completed Example of Workform 7: Recording Staff Tasks: Self-Report Log

A. Location and/or work unit: Ash Branch Reference

B. Date and day of report: Monday 10/4

C. Name: Becky Boyd

D. Job classification: Librarian I

E. Time	F. Task	E. Time	F. Task
9:00	On desk	2:00	Meeting
9:15	On desk/read reviews	2:15	
9:30	→	2:30	
9:45	On desk	2:45	
10:00	Develop bibliography	3:00	Weed/reorder damaged materials
10:15	→	3:15	
10:30	Break	3:30	→
10:45	Develop bibliography	3:45	Break
11:00	→	4:00	On desk
11:15	Create orders	4:15	
11:30	→	4:30	
11:45	→	4:45	
12:00	On desk	5:00	
12:15		5:15	
12:30		5:30	
12:45	→	5:45	→

Recording Staff Tasks: Direct Observation Log, provides a form for recording observations and instructions for gathering observer-reported data. A completed example is shown in figure 13.

This data collection process will probably provide the most accurate data about how staff members are spending their time. However, workers may resent being observed (and perhaps become very resentful if they find out they were observed without their knowledge). The "Hawthorne effect" can also come into play. Named after the famous study done by Harvard Business School professor Elton Mayo at the Hawthorne Plant of the Western Electric Company in Cicero, Illinois, the Hawthorne effect is the phenomenon of workers changing their behavior because they are being observed. It's hard not to become self-conscious or to want to do particularly well if you know you're being watched. Depending upon the situation, this effect may or may not be something to be concerned about. In many library situations the workers are so busy and the work is so routine that those being observed can quickly forget that they are being observed. In other situations, tensions raised by being observed can be much more apparent and influential.

Gathering information on how staff spend their time provides data you can use to refine your numeric analyses. Let's go back to Tree County Public Library's technical services department to see how Bev gathers and uses this data.

<table>
<tr><td>

CASE STUDY

TREE COUNTY PUBLIC LIBRARY TECHNICAL SERVICES

</td><td>

Bev Bingham's first numeric analysis demonstrated that the cataloging workloads had not increased between last year and this year. However, clearly something is not the same. Bev decides to ask the cataloging staff to record how they spend their days by completing Workform 7, Recording Staff Tasks: Self-Report Log.

In reviewing the workforms, Bev discovers that each cataloger spends approximately 5 hours a week in various meetings. She also knows that her staff has been with the library a long time and gets the maximum annual vacation leave—three weeks each. She decides to calculate the actual number of productive hours of cataloging done in an average week.

Using Workform 2, Estimate of Productive Work Hours Available, Bev determines that the 2.5 FTE cataloger positions actually represent 3,608 productive hours per year. To this she adds 735 hours to represent the extra 15 hours per week (for 49 weeks, still allowing for 3 weeks of vacation) to get a total of 4,343 productive hours. To catalog the 27,250 new titles received this year, staff members need an output rate of 6.5 titles per hour, or 9 minutes per title.

</td></tr>
</table>

Comparing Baseline Measures

Baselines give you a snapshot of workload at the point of the measurement. However, real information is not in the baseline itself, but in the comparison of the baseline with another measure of the same

FIGURE 13

Completed Example of Workform 8: Recording Staff Tasks: Direct Observation Log

A. Day of the week: ___Monday___   **B.** Date of observation: ___10/10___   **C.** Location and/or work unit observed: ___Birch Branch Reference___

D. Staff on duty on this date:

1. Name: ___Joe Jones___	Classification: ___Librarian I___
2. Name: ___Mary Morris___	Classification: ___Librarian I___
3. Name: ___Alice Able___	Classification: ___Library Assistant___
4. Name: _____	Classification: _____
5. Name: _____	Classification: _____
6. Name: _____	Classification: _____

Direct Observation Log (Cont.)

E. Time	F. Name/Job Classification	G. Location	H. Task
10:15	Joe Jones	Reference Desk	Patron assistance
10:18	Mary Morris	Reference Desk	Wait work
10:20	Alice Able	Reference work room	Processing new materials
11:30	Joe Jones	Reference Desk	Wait work
11:35	Mary Morris	Reference work room	Selection
11:30	Alice Able	Reference Desk	Patron assistance

workload. The comparison might be among the baselines calculated for multiple work units, as in figure 7 (earlier), to compare performance across various agencies. The comparison might be used to track performance across multiple time periods for a single work unit by comparing the baseline measure with subsequent workload calculations for that same work unit, as in figure 14. On the other hand, it might involve using a baseline to set performance standards for tasks in your library. To use a baseline numeric measure as a performance standard, you would periodically measure the output of individuals doing the task and compare the results with the baselines you develop. Many organizations use their baselines as minimal standards and challenge staff to find ways to "raise the base" as a part of Total Quality Management (TQM) efforts.

Comparing baseline measurements often generates a series of questions and, often, more data gathering and analysis. Look again at figure 7. Why do the clerks at Elm Branch seem to be doing so much more work than the clerks at the other branches? Don't jump to the conclusion that the other clerks are slacking off or that these clerks are particularly productive; gather data that will help identify variables that contribute to the workload disparity.

There could be a whole host of environmental factors that affect the results you are seeing. You might find, for example, that branch size makes a difference. You might find that there are more library customer interactions in some branches than in others or that the mix of materials circulated is different. You might also find out that other parts of the clerk's job are taking more time in some branches than in others. In some locations there might be more work to do filling holds or preparing deliveries or assisting the children's librarian.

The introduction of user self-service can significantly alter your results as well. If you have self-checkout machines in one or more of your libraries, be sure that the circulation numbers for these machines are not included in the output data you are using. Even if you are using only the staff-assisted circulation numbers, self-checkout machines still affect your results. If the self-checkout machines are successful and well received by the public, consider how that affects the typical staff/user interaction at the circulation desk. Users with no problems can use the

FIGURE 14

Ash Branch Workloads

Year	Circulation per FTE
FY 1	110,775
FY 2	113,396
FY 3	115,420
FY 4	119,110

self-checkout machines, users whose cards have stops of one type or another cannot. This means that the proportion of "problem" transactions increases at the circulation desk, and problem transactions take longer because of the resolution time involved. Self-service reserve placement can have similar effects on workload calculations, particularly if some of your service outlets serve communities that are technologically advanced and others serve populations that are less technologically sophisticated.

You might also find out that the statistics you have traditionally kept don't really reflect the total workload of the task you are measuring. For example, if circulation means "books checked out" at your library, circulation data may not be giving you the whole picture. With the advent of automated library consortia, regional or statewide library cards, and liberal policies about where a library customer may return an item, some libraries are now finding that they check in more materials than they check out because the library is a convenient drop-off site. A user might pick up a requested item near where he works but drop it off near his home after he's done with it. If this distinction between checkouts and check-ins looks important in your library, you might want to calculate workloads for them both rather than thinking of checkouts as the only measurement of circulation.

Clearly, developing numeric measurements can lead to as many questions as it answers. Chapter 4, Basic Process Analysis, and chapter 5, Beyond the Basics, will discuss ways to identify and measure the variables that affect numeric measures.

Chapter 4

Basic Process Analysis

MILESTONES

By the time you finish this chapter you will know how to

- determine when to use process analysis
- define the start and stop points of a task
- record the steps in a task
- analyze the data you collect
- understand the difference between input-driven and demand-driven tasks

At its simplest, process analysis is about determining what steps within a task are required to create a measurable output. To do this you must be able to identify four things: the output that is created and measured, the starting point of the task, the typical steps within the task, and the ending point of the task. The numeric analysis discussed in chapter 3 links the number of outputs produced with the level of effort needed to produce them. Process analysis helps you understand how those outputs are produced. Whereas numeric analysis can be done at the activity, task, or step level, process analysis is done on tasks and steps.

> A *task* is a series of steps that converts inputs to outputs.
>
> *Inputs* are the materials, equipment, information, and people needed to carry out the task.
>
> An *output* is the measurable result of a task, the product or service handed to the customer. The customer may be external, one of the library's patrons, for example, or internal, another department or person working within the library.

Choosing to Analyze Process

There are a variety of reasons why library managers might decide that process analysis is the most appropriate approach to use to achieve the goal of their workload analysis project. When an organization is seeking to make changes in its performance, to reduce costs, to improve productivity, or to reallocate staff time, changes are often made in the processes of doing work. Sometimes an activity or task will be eliminated entirely, but more frequently the change will be in the way in which the work is accomplished to achieve the desired outputs. Total quality management (TQM), process reengineering, and continuous improvement initiatives are all about analyzing and changing work processes to improve performance.

The changing nature of library work is driving many libraries to look for different ways of doing things. The introduction of technology into the delivery of direct public service has added a wide range of new activities to the average library's workload. Strategic service planning initiatives such as *The New Planning for Results* process are leading libraries to revise their service offerings to meet the needs of changing communities.[1] Many new activities are being undertaken without additional staffing to support them. Redesigning work processes is one way to release staff hours from current tasks to take on new responsibilities. Process analysis is the starting point for redesigning work.

The impetus behind initiating a workload analysis project can also be a problem that needs to be solved. Backlogs in technical services or reshelving of materials are classic examples of the types of problems that lead library directors to ask, "Isn't there a better way to do this?" Requests for additional staffing to handle increased demands for service are another trigger for looking at how work is done. If you are using numeric performance indicators to monitor your organization, a significant deviation from your established baseline might also prompt you to ask what is going on. Process analysis can provide the answers to these questions.

Deciding What You Need to Know

The first challenge in doing a process analysis is to precisely define the task you want to study. This is not as simple as you might think. Library directors and senior management staff tend to view the organization from a large, cross-functional perspective, a macroview of the work. For them the task of building the collection includes the steps of selecting titles, ordering and receiving the materials, cataloging the titles, and shelving the materials, even though defining the task this way, as figure 15 graphically shows, involves the work of three separate departments within the library.

For the staff involved in doing the work, each of the boxes in figure 15 represents a separate task. For example, the "select titles" step becomes its own task with multiple steps when seen from the perspective

FIGURE 15

Macroview of Building a Collection

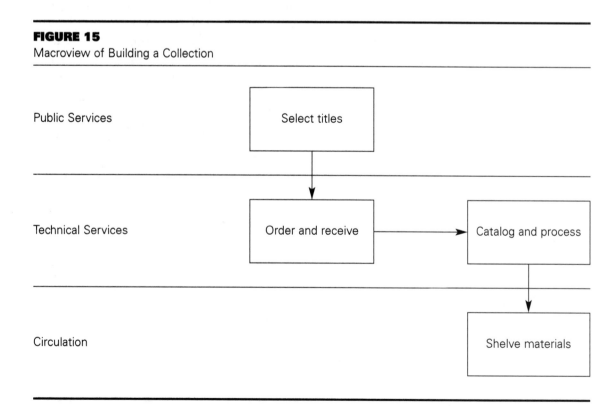

of the public services staff who do the work. Figure 16 shows a microview of the "select titles" step.

A macroprocess, the big picture overview of one of an organization's functions, is made up of hundreds of microprocesses, the employee-level view of the work. Although major organizational restructuring can affect macroprocesses, it is at the microprocess level where significant changes are made.

There is also the fundamental question: "Why is this task done at all? What does it contribute to achieving the library's goals and objectives?" You probably already answered this question before you decided to spend time and money studying an activity or task, but it is not a bad idea to ask and answer it again as you begin to collect data so you can remind yourself of why you continue to do this thing. Every library has its "sacred cow" activities that continue to be done because "we have always done them." Spending time trying to make these activities more productive is a classic case of rearranging the deck chairs on the *Titanic*. You could do it, but why would you? The only legitimate reason is that politics require you to continue.

Define the Start and Stop Points

If you are undertaking a process analysis as a way of solving a problem, it is quite likely that you already have a fair amount of data about the problem. You know what output results from the process and what the measures are for that output. You know who is involved in doing the work. The next step is asking the staff who do the work to describe the steps in the process. However, before you do that you have to be able to tell them where to start and where to end their descriptions of the steps in the task. Does reshelving materials begin when you leave the sorting area with a truck of books, or does it begin with presorting materials onto the truck? Is the final step in processing new materials putting them on a new book truck to be picked up by staff from another department, checking them in to trigger any outstanding reserves, or dropping them off in a delivery area to be distributed?

FIGURE 16
Microview of Selecting Titles

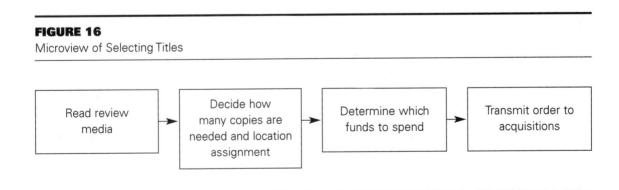

Defining the starting point and ending point of a task is a crucial component of developing data that can be compared across multiple work units. In the same way that a controlled vocabulary ensures comparable data on the amount of effort required to accomplish an output, common starting and ending points provide clear boundaries for the tasks you are assessing. Although you will find variations in the ways individuals perform the same task, by specifying the starting and ending points, you can have confidence that the variations relate to the task you are studying.

The starting and ending points may be predefined by the person in charge of data gathering and communicated to the staff who will be completing the actual data-collection workforms. Alternately, you could have a discussion with the staff who actually do the task to get their input and agreement about when the process starts and stops. In either case, be sure that all of the staff or observers who will be gathering data understand where they should start and stop their reporting of the steps.

Define the Steps in Each Task

Once the boundaries of starting and stopping points have been set, you will need to determine the typical workflow or steps in the task you are studying and agree upon the vocabulary that will be used to describe those steps. Identifying the steps in a task can be done through self-reporting or through one-on-one observation. More information about both mechanisms is in chapter 3. In either case, it is important to identify what *is* done in the process, *not* what should be done. Recording steps from the procedure manual will not tell you how work is actually done. You may be very surprised at the deviations from the procedure manual you discover as you complete your study.

Self-reporting works best for those tasks that are done out of the public eye. Staff can accurately record technical services, administrative activities, and off-desk work as they are performing their work tasks. Observers are valuable in recording public service tasks because it can be disruptive to ask staff to record the steps in a task while they are providing services to the public and because recording the steps from memory after the patron leaves the desk will not provide an accurate or complete picture. You can use Workform 9, Analysis of a Task, to gather data on the steps in a task by self-reporting and observation.

Staff will need training to be able to complete Workform 9 effectively. Following are several key points to emphasize:

It is very important that staff comply with the common starting and stopping points.

The steps reported in the task must be continuous, which means that the end of one step is the starting point for the next step.

Each staff member asked to complete the workform must complete it independently, not in a joint effort with others who do this task nor by copying someone else's list of steps.

Staff will be more likely to comply with these requirements if they are assured that you are not studying their performance, but the work itself. You may find you get better compliance if staff are not required to put their names on the workforms; however, that will preclude your being able to ask them any questions you have as a result of your analysis of the data.

If you are gathering the data through self-reports, every staff member who is responsible for a task within a work unit should be asked to complete the forms. This will give you the most comprehensive picture of how the task is accomplished. If the workform is completed by observers, everyone in the work unit who does the task should be observed through multiple repetitions or at multiple times. An observer will not be able to tell from a single observation if an action is a usual step in the task or a special-case deviation from the normal way the task is done. Multiple observations will provide enough data to determine the typical steps in a task. Figure 17 shows a completed example of one such observation recorded on Workform 9.

Analyzing the Data

Reviewing the completed Workform 9s can provide a wealth of information. Start by reviewing the workforms submitted by each staff member to determine how much commonality there is. You will quite likely find variations in the way each individual completes the task. Analyze why the differences exist. Are some staff doing things others are not? Are the steps the same but the order in which they are done different? Is this difference the result of personal preference, or does it indicate a possible problem? In one technical services process analysis most staff members printed processing slips for newly received materials as they were checked in; one staff member printed them all in a batch at the end of her work. Questioning the reason for the difference, the project manager found that the one staff member's work area was too small to house a printer. Rearranging the furniture saved nearly half an hour of double handling of materials for each order the staff member checked in.

Sometimes the differences that appear to exist in the steps within a task turn out to be a matter of vocabulary—the terms staff use for steps—rather than the actual work itself. For example, what one staff member may call "updating item records" another may refer to as "changing collections." If you think that different terms are being used

FIGURE 17

Completed Example of Workform 9: Analysis of a Task (Observation)

A. ☐ Self-report ☒ Observer report

B. Location and/or work unit: Main Library reference desk

C. Name and job classification of person performing the task: Mary Morris, Librarian I

D. Task: Selecting materials—choosing materials and verifying and preparing orders

E. What gets counted: Number of titles ordered

F. Starting point of task: Gather review materials

G. List the steps involved in sequence

1. Read review

2. Check online catalog for duplication

3. Complete order card, including number to order and suggested distribution

4.

5.

6.

7.

8.

9.

10.

H. End point of task: Send order cards to department head for review and approval

I. Is there anything you would change in this process?   ☐ Yes   ☒ No

If yes, attach a separate sheet to this workform outlining your suggestions for changes.

for the same work, it will be worth your time to create a controlled vocabulary describing each step of the task and then to repeat the data-collection process. This will ensure that you have an accurate and complete picture of the steps within the task to use as the basis for any decision making.

The most effective way to develop a controlled vocabulary to describe the steps within a task or process is to ask a group of staff members who perform the task to review the data you gathered on Workform 9 and recommend terms to be used for each step in the task. During the course of this discussion, the variations in the way different staff approach the task will probably become clearer to staff and managers alike. Once the staff has agreed on a set of steps, record the results on Workform 4, Standard Terms in Our Library for Tasks and Steps.

Preliminary Review

After you have a sense of the common steps in the task, review each and ask yourself if these are the appropriate steps for this task. Is each of these steps necessary? The steps in a task can be either value-added or nonvalue-added steps. Value-added steps contribute to customer satisfaction. They add something to the output of the process that the customer values—something the customer would miss if they were eliminated. Nonvalue-added steps generally get added to a process to satisfy some person in the organization other than the primary customer of the process.

Consider these steps in the physical processing of a book in an Illinois public library:

1. Property stamp the top edge with the library's name.
2. Property stamp the library's name in the gutter on page 36.
3. Apply call number label to spine.
4. Add clear tape over the call number label.

Does each of these steps add value? The customers of physical processing are the staff and the public. Circulation uses the top stamp to visually check that the returned book belongs to this library without needing to open the book. Staff and the public use the call number label to find the book on the shelves. The tape over the call number label increases the visibility of the label by keeping it clean and keeping it from peeling off, two things the staff and public value. Who uses the property stamp on page 36? Who would notice if it were eliminated? Don't assume you know the answer to questions like this, instead, ask the customers of the process if their work would be affected if the step were eliminated. If the answer is no, eliminate the step.

Even if the answer is "Yes, elimination of the step would occasionally affect us," you may still decide to eliminate the step. You have to balance the effect of step elimination against the cost, in time or dollars, of continuing to perform the step. The director of the Illinois library asked who used the stamp on page 36 and was told that it mattered to the circulation staff. A circulation staff member said she used the page 36 stamps when books were returned without their bar codes and with the top-edge stamp erased. Asking how often that happened, she could discover only one incident that anyone could remember. The step was eliminated.

Question any step that is done because "they require it." Ask who "they" are, then question that person or group about the requirement. Often the target group is surprised to hear about their supposed requirement. One technical services department in a large public library invested the equivalent of nearly a full-time staff member in manually recording, collecting, and reporting monthly statistics on the steps in their operation because "the library board requires it." By studying the flow of statistics from technical services to the monthly board report, it was discovered that the statistics were never presented to the board. Indeed, they were never used at all by either technical services managers or any other library administrator.

In another example, the interlibrary loan department of a state library ended its processing of outgoing materials by tying the bundles of materials with string before sending them down to the shipping dock because "the dock requires it." A new interlibrary loan supervisor, studying the process to understand his operation better, discovered that the first thing the loading dock staff did with materials they received from interlibrary loan was to cut the string. When the ILL supervisor asked the dock staff why the interlibrary loan department tied the bundles, the dock staff said they didn't know, that it must be something they needed to do in interlibrary loan.

Seemingly small steps are sometimes added to a process without considering the number of times that small step is performed. An individual step may be of short duration, but if it is added to a high-volume activity like circulation or technical services, it can quickly consume a significant amount of staff time. Challenge the statement: "It's not a problem; it doesn't take very long anyway." A five-second step that is done 250,000 times a year adds up to more than 347 hours of staff time—more than 43 days of work for a person working an eight-hour day.

Ask yourself if you understand the reason for each step. Are these reasons valid, or are they based on some previous set of circumstances that no longer applies? Any step being done because "we have always done it that way" or because "that is how I was trained to do it" should be questioned. Library staffs are very creative at making do in difficult circumstances. We work around space limitations, equipment limitations, even the physical limitations of staff members when they are ill or injured. Unfortunately, these work-arounds, developed for a specific set of temporary conditions, all too often become permanent steps in a process long after the original reason has disappeared.

Are the steps being done in the right order? To answer this question you may want to string together multiple Workform 9s and look at the larger picture as well as at the individual steps each person does. As with the statistics and interlibrary loan examples, the individual tasks may make logical sense until you follow the work from one work unit to another. Look for handoffs from one unit or person to another and for outputs that are handled multiple times by a person or work group. The more handoffs, the greater opportunity you will find for improvement.

As you can see, just a cursory view of completed Workform 9s can generate an amazing number of questions and help you identify a number of reasonable steps you can take quickly to simplify and streamline processes in your library. When you find these steps, do them. Then evaluate the results of your changes to determine if you have achieved your objectives. Remember that you started this process analysis with an objective in mind, such as eliminating backlogs, reducing the number of steps or people involved in a process, or reducing the time a process takes. Sometimes it doesn't take radical reorganization to solve a problem. The cumulative effect of small changes can be powerful.

Time Factor

Some steps in a task take considerably more time than others. If your objective is to reduce the time or expense it takes to accomplish a task, you'll want to focus your attention on the steps or tasks that take the longest or are done the most frequently. You can ask staff to help you identify those steps by completing Workform 10, Time Spent on an Input-Driven Task, or Workform 11, Time Spent on a Demand-Driven Task. These are two separate workforms because there are typically two types of tasks in libraries: those that are input driven and those that are demand driven.

Input-driven tasks are those tasks where you have a known number of things to accomplish, and the speed with which you accomplish them is controlled by the resources you assign to the task. Technical services, materials shelving, interagency delivery services, shelf reading, weeding, Web page development, and programming are all examples of input-driven tasks. With these tasks you have a reasonable amount of control over how many of these things you try to accomplish in any given period of time. (See, for example, figure 18.) If you have only two hours a week to work on the Web pages, you are probably not going to expect to produce ten new pages a week. If you are willing to tolerate occasional backlogs, you can assign enough library page hours to shelve 1,200 items a day, even if your daily circulation exceeds 2,000 some days.

Demand-driven tasks are less predictable than are input-driven tasks. You prepare for an expected level of customer demand, but you don't have any real control over whether that level of demand materializes. The demand for the service you offer may be more than you antici-

FIGURE 18

Completed Example of Workform 10: Time Spent on an Input-Driven Task

A. Location and/or work unit: __Ash Branch__

B. Name of person performing the task: __Tressa Jones__

C. Task: __Processing hold materials for pickup__

D. Step	E. Start Time	F. End Time	G. Elapsed Time	H. Number Completed	I. Output Rate (G/H or H/G)
1. Receive and organize hold materials	12:45	1:15	30 min.	35	1.16 per minute or 70 per hour
2. Phone or e-mail patrons	1:15	1:50	35 min.	35	1 per minute or 60 per hour
3. Label materials with patron names	1:50	2:10	20 min.	35	1.75 per minute or 105 per hour
4. Arrange materials being held on book truck by patron last name	2:10	2:20	10 min.	35	3.5 per minute or 210 per hour
5.					
6.					
7.					
8.					
9.					
10.					

pated; it may be less. Circulation, reference services, employee recruitment, meeting room and PC usage, help desk support, and technology repairs are all examples of demand-driven tasks. Lines at the reference desk or busy signals when customers call the help desk indicate greater than anticipated demand. If you have circulation clerks standing around behind the desk with nothing to do, it means you probably have staffed for more services than you are being asked to deliver.

Input-Driven Tasks

Input-driven tasks are easier to study and to change than demand-driven tasks because you control the factors that contribute to performance: the number of outputs you expect and the level of effort expended in creating those outputs. You control how many books are purchased through the size of your budget. You control how many materials are moved in your delivery system by the size of your trucks and the number of staff you assign to the task.

Input-driven tasks usually involve applying a series of steps to a volume of outputs. Typically each step is completed for a number of outputs before the next step is initiated. Library pages usually shelve books by the truckload rather than one at a time. Catalogers send their newly cataloged titles on to the next station in technical services in batches. Even if the volume of output is only one item, a single Web page developed during a two-hour period, the work itself is characterized by the fact that the person doing it had control over it. If the Web page had taken only 45 minutes to complete, the developer could have begun a second page during the two-hour work window.

The steps in an input-driven task can be identified and timed as discrete actions. Workform 10, Time Spent on an Input-Driven Task, provides staff with a way to record the time they spend on each step in a task and to indicate how many measurable outputs were handled during that step. Figure 18 is a completed example of Workform 10. The steps listed in column D of the workform are the same steps identified for this activity in item G on Workform 9. Dividing the elapsed time spent on each step by the number of outputs handled during that time gives you the output rate. Reviewing the output rates for the steps will help you quickly identify the steps in the process that take the most time.

CASE STUDY

TREE COUNTY PUBLIC LIBRARY TECHNICAL SERVICES

Bev Bingham's numeric analyses show that the catalogers need an output rate of 6.5 titles per hour or 9 minutes per title to avoid cataloging backlogs. She meets with the catalogers to discuss her findings and explore why they think the backlog is growing. The catalogers think it takes less than 9 minutes per title for print materials, but they believe that nonprint materials take longer. The catalogers agree to complete Workform 10, Time Spent on an Input-Driven Task, for the next two weeks to develop information about how long each format of material takes to catalog.

Bev and the staff discuss the steps they should record in the activity of cataloging. Using Workform 9, Analysis of a Task, as a starting point for the discussion, the catalogers identify the following steps:

searching OCLC

editing found records

transferring data to the library's local system

running an authority control check

saving the authorized records

The cataloging group is also responsible for entering item information into the local system for each piece of material and correcting database errors found and reported by public services.

After discussing how to collect the data they need, the catalogers and Bev agree that all of the steps from searching OCLC through saving the record in the local system can be aggregated into a single step they will call "cataloging." Cataloging will be tracked by format—print and nonprint. Item input and database corrections will be the other two steps they record. Item input will be tracked by format as well. The starting point for the task will be the arrival of materials from acquisitions or public services (database errors) and the ending point will be sending the materials to the processor.

The results startle everyone. Print titles average 7 minutes each to complete; nonprint titles average 20 minutes. That means the 2,500 nonprint titles added with the budget increase require 833 hours of additional cataloging effort. Bev's deal with the director only produced 735 hours. Her decision to make the nonprint materials the highest priority for cataloging exacerbated the backlog because each 20 minutes spent on a nonprint title meant three print titles weren't being done.

Once you know which steps are the most time consuming, you can begin to look for ways to reduce the time. Think about the following: Why are these steps the most time consuming? Is there some way you can speed them by changing the physical environment, for example, moving supplies closer or changing the location of equipment or furniture? Is there some form of mechanization or automation you could use, a computer printer rather than a typewriter, preprinted labels rather than inkpads and stamps? Could you download a file from one computer to another rather than updating multiple databases separately? Can you have some of the steps performed elsewhere? Could you, for instance, buy materials partially preprocessed? Ask the people who completed the workform why a step takes so long and if they have any suggestions about how it might be done faster. You may be impressed by the suggestions you'll get from the people who have to do the work every day.

Demand-Driven Tasks

Demand-driven tasks are usually characterized by steps that are completed in sequence for each output of the task. A reference transaction may include the steps of greeting the user, conducting a reference interview to ascertain the need, supplying a resource that will answer the query, and confirming that the patron is satisfied with the result. This task is generally completed with one user before the next request for service is handled. Checking out materials, collecting fines, and instructing users on the Internet or electronic databases one-on-one are all examples of this type of service.

Assessing the time spent on demand-driven tasks focuses on discovering the average time to complete one occurrence of the task. Rather than measuring how long the reference librarian spends greeting the user or conducting the interview portion of the transaction, you want to know what the average time spent per reference question is. The challenge is that most public service points offer a variety of service outputs to the public. For example, staff at reference desks answer directional queries as well as reference questions. Circulation staff check out books, receive fines, register patrons for library cards, and answer questions about policies and procedures. The service mix is an element of the workload assessment. A reference desk staff that answers primarily directional queries may appear to accomplish more per hour worked than a desk staff that answers reference questions. Part of assessing demand-driven tasks is to be sure that you can distinguish which types of services are being timed.

Workform 11, Time Spent on Demand-Driven Tasks, will help you develop information about how long the average activity takes. Although staff on public service desks in libraries that are not very busy can complete this workform, during busy periods you will probably want to use an observer to record this information. (See chapter 3 for more information on collecting information through observation.) The information will be more accurate, and the data collection will have less of an impact on your public. Figure 19 shows an example of a completed Workform 11.

What can you do with this data once you have collected it? Well, the first thing you can ask yourself is if the mix of tasks seems right. If the study period shows that the reference staff spends 95 percent of its time answering reference and directional queries and only 5 percent of the time on Internet instruction, is that the service model your library's goals and objectives describe? Does the amount of time an average transaction takes seem reasonable? If it is taking as long to answer directional queries (for example, where the copier is) as it is to answer reference questions, something is wrong. Are the tasks listed appropriate for the staff covered by the report? For example, have you just discovered that the circulation staff in one of the branches is doing Internet instruction?

Review all of the Workform 11s for staff working at the same desk. Do you see a pattern in the division of labor? Are some staff members doing one type of work while others are focusing on different tasks? This may be completely reasonable. For example, your policies may

FIGURE 19

Completed Example of Workform 11: Time Spent on a Demand-Driven Task

A. Location and/or work unit: ___Ash Branch___

B. Task: ___Circulation service at desk___

C. Name of person recording/observed: ___Mary Meyers___

D. Day and time of record/observation: ___Thursday, 10/10/02___

E. Step	F. Start Time	G. End Time	H. Elapsed Time
1. checkout for a patron	10:10	10:12	2 min.
2. checkout for a patron	10:15	10:16	1 min.
3. checkout for a patron	10:17	10:19	2 min.
4. register new user	10:25	10:29	4 min.
5. checkout for a patron	10:29	10:30	1 min.
6. checkout for a patron	10:31	10:33	2 min.
7. complete new user input	10:34	10:38	4 min.
8. checkout for a patron	10:45	10:46	1 min.
9. register new user	10:50	10:52	2 min.
10. complete new user input	10:53	10:58	5 min.

Summary of Steps

I. Step Type	J. Number of Occurrences	K. Total Elapsed Time	L. Time per Occurrence (K/J)
1. checkout for a patron	6	9 min.	1.5 min.
2. register new user	2	6 min.	3.0 min.
3. complete new user input	2	9 min.	4.5 min.

limit the number of people at the desk who handle money. It may also be indicative of a need for further training or a values problem. Perhaps you are seeing the results of staff that don't believe they should have to do a particular task.

As with Workform 9, you can learn a lot by just looking for patterns and discrepancies in these workforms. Whenever something strikes you as interesting or unusual, ask about it. Sometimes you find a problem that can be easily corrected, sometimes you find a reasonable explanation, and sometimes you find that the question will lead you to further data gathering and more analysis. The next chapter provides additional tools for more in-depth analysis of data.

NOTE

1. Sandra Nelson, *The New Planning for Results: A Streamlined Approach* (Chicago: American Library Assn., 2001).

Chapter 5

Beyond the Basics

MILESTONES

By the time you finish this chapter you will know how to

- calculate and use numeric averages

- understand data spreads

- interpret percentages and percentiles

- identify transport, storage, and approval points in activities

- map the flow of work activities

Chapters 3 and 4 described basic techniques for calculating numeric measures and analyzing work processes. You can learn a lot about the work processes in your library and the workloads of the staff with these basic tools. In many instances, the basic data-gathering techniques and the information they provide will be sufficient for making the decisions you need to make.

Libraries that are implementing continuous improvement programs, libraries finding significant variances in the baseline numeric measures they have developed, or those that are using workload targets and results as part of a performance-based evaluation program may want to go beyond the basics to more sophisticated numerical analyses or more detailed process analyses. This chapter will introduce you to techniques for doing more in-depth analyses.

Analyzing Numeric Measures

Numeric baselines give you a snapshot of workloads at the point of the measurement. However, comparing a baseline with another measure of the same workload can provide additional valuable information. The comparison might be among the baselines calculated for multiple work units, as in figure 7 in chapter 3, or it might be the baseline measure compared with subsequent workload measures calculated for the same work unit, as in figure 20. Remember, as you learned in chapter 3, if you are planning to compare multiple baselines or to compare baselines with subsequent measures, the data collected must represent the same steps in the same tasks to be validly comparable.

In many if not most cases, you will have to decide what is an acceptable workload and what indicates that further probing is needed. There is no right or wrong or good or bad workload, and there are no national standards for library workloads. You will have to decide whether the variances you find are acceptable for your library. That will probably involve finding out if there are any reasons, other than past practice, for the variances. You will have to decide whether there should be a standard, and, if so, what that standard should be. You can-

FIGURE 20

Ash Branch Workloads by Fiscal Year

Year	Circulation per FTE
FY 1	110,775
FY 2	113,396
FY 3	115,420
FY 4	119,110

not make these decisions until you have collected the basic data and employed some basic data analysis techniques on it as described in chapter 3.

Once you've developed several sets of workload measures you want to compare, you can use a variety of techniques to analyze the data. Each of the following techniques provides a simple way to look at what you've found and to consider what it might mean. Think of these techniques as being like the dashboard indicators on your car. The exact location of the needle on your oil pressure gauge or temperature gauge is not as important (unless it's in the red) as the relative location of the indicator. If it stays about the same, you can assume that things are normal. If it moves significantly, that's an indication that you need to probe further to find the problem.

Averages

A basic way to compare workload data is to look at average levels of productivity. Be aware that there are three types of averages and that people are often imprecise in their use of the term *average*. For example, people frequently are talking about the arithmetic mean when they use the term average. The *mean* is the sum of all numbers in a series divided by the number of numbers in the series. For example, figure 21 shows that the mean of the circulation per FTE circulation clerk is 33,958.

The *median* is the other type of average that can be useful in your analysis. It is the number in the middle of a data series. If the series consists of an odd number of values, the median is easy to find: there will be an even number of values both above and below it. If the series

FIGURE 21

Mean Circulation per FTE

Branch	FY Circulation	Number of FTE Circulation Clerks	Annual Circulation per FTE
Ash	113,396	4.0	28,349
Birch	104,461	3.5	29,846
Elm	176,780	4.0	44,195
Fir	112,848	4.0	28,212
Maple	330,464	8.0	41,308
Oak	203,472	5.5	36,995
Pine	100,797	3.5	28,799
Total			237,704

237,704 total circulation per FTE/7 branches =
33,958 mean circulation per FTE

consists of an even number of values, you simply add the two numbers in the middle and divide by 2 to get the median value. For example, if 56 and 58 were the two numbers in the middle of an even-numbered series, the median would be 57.

The mean can be distorted if there are outliers, or values that are considerably higher or lower than the other values in the series. Therefore, it's often more descriptive and accurate to use the median rather than the mean. In figure 22 the Birch Branch's circulation per FTE is the median of this set of branch statistics because three branches had higher and three had lower circulation per FTE.

Another way to deal with the distortion that values that vary greatly can cause is to throw out the highest and lowest values. The disadvantage of this approach, however, is losing the information that showing the whole range of values can provide.

The third type of average is the mode. The *mode* is simply that value that appears most often. This sort of average is usually not used in analyzing library data because the data doesn't typically array itself in a way that would make it useful to look at it in this way.

Statisticians have a more technical term for looking at averages: measuring central tendency. While that might sound dauntingly technical, it is really something we're quite familiar with. Most evaluation and grading systems have built into them the concept of average and the concept that values can be above and below this point. Library managers usually think about workload and productivity in the same way. They use the data to get a picture of what's going on and ask the question "What is the most common or average level of work that's being done?"

Data Spread

Closely related to the idea of averages is the idea of the range or spread of data. Again, looking at our branch circulation example in figure 22, we can see that the range of circulation per clerk is from 28,212 to

FIGURE 22
Median Circulation per FTE

Branch	FY Circulation	Circulation Clerks	Circulation per FTE	
Elm	176,780	4.0	44,195	
Maple	330,464	8.0	41,308	
Oak	203,472	5.5	36,995	
Birch	**104,461**	**3.5**	**29,846**	**Median**
Pine	100,797	3.5	28,799	
Ash	113,396	4.0	28,349	
Fir	112,848	4.0	28,212	

44,195. This is a spread (or difference) of 15,983 circulations per person per year. Just a quick look at the numbers tells you that this is more than half of the lowest figure. That seems like a lot. However, if you divide the spread by 2,080, the nominal number of hours a forty-hour-a-week clerk works in a year, the difference is about 8 circulations an hour. This might not seem significant, but the range of circulations *per hour worked* is 14 to 21. How do you think about this without feeling like you're going in circles? You use other techniques to provide a context for the data you are reviewing.

Percentages and Percentiles

Sometimes, as you saw in the preceding examples, just looking at numbers, even when you're comparing them, doesn't provide enough information to arrive at meaningful conclusions. Numbers usually need some sort of context. One of the most useful forms of context is provided by the use of percentages. *Percentages* show the relative size of two or more numbers. Most people are familiar with percentages (a 4 percent wage increase, a 25 percent discount), but they often make mistakes in computing or analyzing percentages.

What can you find out about the range of circulation productivity? By calculating percentages, you find that the top of the range (for Elm Branch) is 1.57 times or 157 percent of the bottom (for Fir Branch).

$$44,195 / 28,212 = 1.57 \text{ or } 157\% \text{ of the bottom}$$

Done another way, you can find out that the top of the range is 57% larger than the bottom of the range. Since 50 percent is half, you know that the highest producing branch clerks are getting half again as much work done as the lowest producing clerks.

$$(44,195 - 28,212)/28,212 = 57\% \text{ higher than the bottom}$$

Percentages are also very useful in looking at change over time. If the circulation at the branches is going up, you would probably see that as a positive trend; if it's going down, you would see that as negative. For example, in figure 23, the percentage of change is calculated using the following formula:

$$(B - A)/A$$
or new value minus old value divided by old value

Again, as with all of our data collection and analysis, you need to dig deeper to find out what variables may be contributing to the differences you see. Even though percentages are useful in data analysis, be careful how you use them in presenting data.

Base numbers can be so small that the change relationships are meaningless. For example, if the productivity of a particularly detail-oriented

FIGURE 23

Percentage of Change

Branch	A. FY 01 Circulation per FTE	B. FY 02 Circulation per FTE	C. % Change
Ash	15,292	28,349	85%
Birch	29,644	29,846	1%
Elm	49,773	44,195	−13%
Fir	26,424	28,212	7%
Maple	43,130	41,308	−4%
Oak	36,097	36,995	2%
Pine	27,965	28,799	3%
Mean	32,618	33,958	4%

cataloger goes from 1 book per hour to 2, that's a 100 percent increase—but still not the level of productivity you probably want.

Failing to identify the proper base number weakens your argument. Double check or practice on numbers where you can easily see the relationship. Think about how you're trying to make your argument or present your data to determine whether you want to talk in terms of percentage increases, percentage decreases, or percentages as parts of a whole. See which sounds most persuasive or effective.

There may be times when the numbers will be dramatic and should be used instead of percentages. For example, if a library circulates 7 million items a year and decides to stop stamping due dates in the books and to stop crossing off these dates when the books are returned as part of an effort to reduce repetitive motion injuries, they will be eliminating 14 million repetitive motions. That's an impressive number in anyone's book.

Understand the difference between percentages, percentage points, and the numbers they relate to. Consider this statement, "Last year I spent 18 percent of my materials budget on AV materials. This year I plan on spending 20 percent. Therefore, I have had a 2 percent increase." Is this right? No, and it is important for you to understand why. In reality, the difference is 11 percent [(20% − 18%)/18% = 11%]. The dollar difference and absolute difference will depend, in addition, on the dollar amounts being discussed. Eighteen percent of a $500,000 materials budget is more than 20 percent of a $375,000 budget.

Data can also be analyzed in terms of where it falls relative to other data below it. The median position is the same as the 50th percentile. Half of the data is above this point, and half is below it. The 25th percentile is the number below which 25 percent of the cases occur, and the 75th percentile is the number below which 75 percent of the cases occur. This sort of comparative information can be used for both internal and external comparisons.

Within a library system, workload data can be analyzed and compared to see if the range seems acceptable. Looking at the circulation productivity of the seven branches shown in figure 24, you see a fairly tight pattern. With this sort of analysis there will be half the values above the median line and half below, but what we see is that the half below are not very far below, while those above are much farther above.

Multivariate Analysis

The multivariate analysis technique simply looks at more than one variable at a time. Looking at the data and presenting the data in this manner allows you to investigate and display relationships. In figure 24, the clerks at the Elm Branch seem to be doing much more work than the clerks at the other branches. A number of variables may contribute to this workload disparity. Don't take these numbers at face value and leap to conclusions about your staff's productivity. Instead, identify the variables, gather data on them, and use the data and your analysis to make an informed assessment of the situation.

FIGURE 24

Graphic Comparison of Circulation

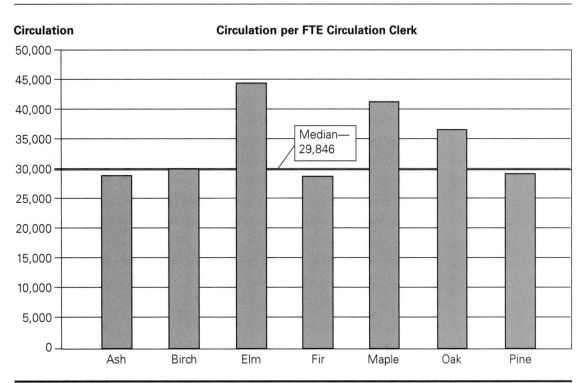

The first challenge in conducting a multivariate analysis is to identify the variables that might be affecting your results. Since you are studying how many outputs are produced with a specific level of effort, start by looking at the variables that affect the time spent doing the work. Questions to ask include:

1. Are there tasks within the activity being studied that themselves could be widely variant? If you are uncomfortable with the variance you find in a set of numeric measures, you may need to study that activity at the task or step levels. For example, in the activity of circulation, there could be tasks for registering patrons, checking the shelves for on-hold books, and calling customers to let them know their hold books are available. Check the statistics for these tasks if you have them. If there are disparities among these statistics for the branches, you may have discovered at least a partial explanation for the variation you see. Using the techniques described in chapter 3 to collect more detailed data about these task outputs will help you gather the information you need for a multivariate analysis.

2. Are there delays built into the processes you are studying that are not separately measured? Look particularly for storage points, approval points, or quality checkpoints in the process.

   Storage points can add time to a process because they generally involve handling materials multiple times.

   Approval points can add time to a process because the processing usually stops while waiting for approval.

   Quality checkpoints are a particular type of approval point.

   While error reduction is an important goal, in many libraries the time spent checking for possible errors far outweighs the amount of time it would take to correct the errors if they were discovered later. Collecting information on the length of the delays introduced will provide data for a multivariate analysis. Workform 13, Workflow Chart, described later in this chapter, will help you identify delay points in a process.

3. Are there environmental factors that affect the results you are seeing? You might find, for example, that branch size makes a difference. You might find that there are more library customer interactions in some branches than in others. On the other hand, you may discover that the mix of materials circulated is different and handling differences can account for the variation in workload results. Does the staff always check audio books to ensure that all of the parts are included whenever an audio book circulates? If so, staff at a branch with a heavy audio-book circulation will take longer to complete an average circulation transaction. Other envi-

ronmental factors could include inconvenient access to needed supplies, overly full bookshelves that make reshelving difficult, crowded aisles, or inappropriate furniture (shelving CDs spine out in book shelves, for example, instead of face forward in media shelving). Identifying the environmental variables that might be affecting your results can take a bit of creativity. Have an observer watch the task and look for possible problems. Ask the staff doing the work what makes the task harder than they think it needs to be. Be sensitive to the implications of what you see and hear.

After you develop a set of numeric calculations for the variant factors you identify, putting your original results and your new data set together in a chart can provide more information about your operations. Adding rankings, which means assigning numbers *1* through *n* (with *1* being the highest and *n* being the lowest for each variable) makes it easier to read and compare the information provided. For example, as shown in figure 25, although the Fir branch ranks last in circulation per FTE, it is the median for holds searched per FTE.

Obviously, environmental factors are not as easily represented by calculated results. However, you may still be able to add information on environmental factors to your other results to improve your understanding of the results. In figure 26 the number of CDs shelved per hour is charted with the availability of specialized shelving for the materials, demonstrating a clear relationship between appropriate shelving and shelving results.

Other Factors to Consider

You might find that the statistics you have traditionally kept don't really reflect the total workload of the task or activity you are measuring. For example, if the number of reference questions answered has been your means of measuring work done at the reference desk, you might be

FIGURE 25

Ranking Numeric Results

Branch	Circulation/ FTE	Rank	Holds Searched/FTE	Rank
Elm	44,195	1	9,720	2
Maple	41,308	2	5,054	6
Oak	36,995	3	10,464	1
Birch	29,846	4	8,307	3
Pine	28,799	5	4,665	7
Ash	28,349	6	6,024	5
Fir	28,212	7	6,300	4

FIGURE 26

Ranking Nonnumeric Factors

Branch	CDs Reshelved/Hour	Rank	CD Shelving Available
Elm	65	1	Y
Maple	60	2	Y
Oak	58	3	Y
Birch	42	4	Some
Pine	30	5	N
Ash	28	6	N
Fir	27	7	N

missing much of what people working at that desk do during the time they are there. In many libraries, in addition to answering questions, reference desk staff sign people up to use PCs, show people how to load and use microform readers, collect payments for copies, schedule meeting rooms, place holds or interlibrary loan requests for library users, and so on. If answering reference questions is only part of what they do, then the numeric measurement is incomplete and, as a result, misleading.

You also might find that reference desk staff answer several different kinds of questions and only count the ones that you define as "reference." What happens to the directional or informational questions? They take time, too, if the reference staff answers them. If statistics for these other questions aren't captured, the numeric measurement for reference staff tasks is incomplete.

Just thinking through what you really measure and why you measure it may begin to reveal some issues you can address immediately. You might find yourself wondering why you need librarians with degrees to answer directional questions or to take meeting room reservations. If you find that a large percentage of their time is spent doing this, you will undoubtedly want to rethink your staffing patterns and work assignments.

Detailed Process Analysis

Using Workform 9, Analysis of a Task, to gather process data creates a list of the steps in a task. Simply reviewing those steps and asking the basic questions included in chapter 4 can provide useful information that will help you restructure and improve processes in your library. You can use Workform 9 repeatedly in studying a task to develop increasingly narrow views of work processes. Do this by selecting a step from a task you are studying, treat that step as if it were a task, and have staff complete Workform 9 again to analyze the components of the step under review. The types of steps you will want to study in depth are the ones that take a significant amount of time or that seem to be overly complex.

Whenever you have lists of steps to study, there are likely to be a number of questions you'll find yourself asking. Two of the most common questions are, "What does it cost to do this?" and "Isn't there some way we can do this faster?" Let's assume that you eliminated the nonvalue-added steps when you found them and that you are now working with steps that add value to the output. Remember, value-added steps contribute something that enhances the customer's satisfaction with the output of the process. Nonvalue-added steps do not; indeed, they are generally added to a process to satisfy some person in the organization other than the primary customer of the process.

In any task, some steps take more time than others. If your objective is to reduce the time or expense it takes to accomplish an activity, you'll want to focus your attention on the steps or tasks that take the longest or are done the most frequently. You can identify those steps by reviewing completed copies of Workform 10, Time Spent on an Input-Driven Task, or Workform 11, Time Spent on a Demand-Driven Task.

Let's look at how Tree County Public Library's technical services staff responded to the discovery that nonprint materials take so much longer than print materials to catalog.

CASE STUDY

TREE COUNTY PUBLIC LIBRARY TECHNICAL SERVICES

Once they get over the shock of discovering that nonprint materials take three times as long to catalog as print materials do, Bev and her staff focus their attention on why this is so and how to reduce the time.

The catalogers complete another round of Workforms 9 and 10, this time using the more-detailed steps they had previously aggregated into the term "cataloging." They study both print and nonprint materials, planning to use the results of the print materials study as a baseline against which they can compare the nonprint results.

They discover that it takes longer to edit nonprint records they found on OCLC and that it takes longer to enter the item information for nonprint materials. They understand why the item information for nonprint materials takes longer because most nonprint materials have multiple parts and the library's policy is to put a bar code on each part separately and enter each. The reason for the editing variance is not as clear. So they study it again, in even greater detail. They learn just how frequently a cataloger actually views the credits in a video as a part of the bibliographic record edit process. Matching a book to an OCLC record takes much less time than matching a video with Tree County's cataloging policies and procedures.

The question that Bev faces now is clear. Did the step of viewing the video credits add enough value to users of the database to warrant the time expended? Yes, viewing the credits was the bibliographically correct thing to do to determine that the MARC record correctly described all of the contributors and players. However, did it really enhance the customer's satisfaction with the output? Did Tree County's library users search the online catalog for videos by producer, director, writer, or supporting players frequently enough that the cataloging staff needed to verify information that didn't appear on the box?

Studying Public Service Desks

As noted in chapter 3, studying the steps taken to deliver service at a public service desk can be challenging because of the diversity of tasks that can take place. Nevertheless, it can be done if you aggregate the tasks you study into a limited number or if you focus very narrowly on one or two tasks and record those only when they occur.

At public service desks it sometimes makes more sense to record what happens during a specific time window rather than sampling what each staff member is doing, as Workform 8, Recording Staff Time: Direct Observation Log, is designed to do. Workform 12, Time Spent on Public Desks, is designed to help you record the steps at a public desk continuously for a period of time. It is very similar to Workform 11, Time Spent on a Demand-Driven Task, but Workform 12 has been slightly redesigned to ease data gathering in a fast-moving environment. Workform 11 could be used by staff to record their own activities; Workform 12 is designed to be used only by an observer.

CASE STUDY

TREE COUNTY PUBLIC LIBRARY REFERENCE SERVICES

The next time the advisory group gets together, Zeke tells them what he learned when he looked at the reference statistics branch by branch. The numbers have dropped at some branches and risen at others. He never put much faith in the door-count statistics, but he looked at those, too. What he found was supportive of the comment Susan made: both reference and attendance were up at the two branches that served the poorest areas of the county.

Susan looks thoughtful as he makes his presentation. "You know," she says, "that really ties in with what we're trying to clarify here. We're doing a lot more for these library users than just answering reference questions—we provide PCs and help with using them; a place to do homework; a warm, dry, free place to spend the afternoon; even bathrooms—to people who don't have a lot. I guess that explains why we have more difficult interactions, too. A lot of our patrons are tired, hungry, fed up, strung out . . . no wonder we feel so tired and stressed!"

At this revelation, the group quickly concludes that they need to gather information about reference desk work at each branch. The advisory group decides the data will be more accurate and collecting it will be easier on the desk staff if observers do the collecting using Workform 12. By this time they were very aware that they provided demand-driven service!

The discussion also results in a decision to have a meeting with all reference staff to discuss the project with them and to answer questions. The advisory group realizes that the project is pointless without good data and that good data can't be collected if staff don't understand the project's purpose.

Capturing data on public service steps can be challenging, but it can be done. Holding an information meeting at this point in the project will ameliorate concerns staff might have about the decision to gather data through observation.

Following the Flow of the Work

The time it takes to produce an output sometimes involves more than just the actual time spent on steps in a task. Approval points, storage time, and transporting materials from place to place can also add time to a process, particularly if you are studying processes at the macro level.

Workform 13, Workflow Chart provides a way to capture information on process points that might not be revealed in Workforms 9–11. In addition to the operational steps the staff identified, in this workform you may also list steps that are a part of the process but didn't appear in the staff workforms, such as moving new materials from receiving to acquisitions or holding orders for the reference supervisor to review and approve. Once you get all of the steps listed in chronological order, mark each of them as an operation, transport, approval, or storage step based on the following definitions:

An *operation* step is one is which staff work directly with an input.

A *transport* step involves the movement of inputs from one place to another during a process.

An *approval* step is one in which no further steps are taken in the process until after the approval is given.

A *storage* step involves setting inputs aside at the end of one step until some other step is completed.

Marking the workform to indicate what types of steps are in the process provides you with a graphical view of the possible built-in delay points.

Another way you might use this data is to diagram the flow of the processes you are studying. Figure 27 shows a completed Workform 13 for a macroprocess overview of technical services. This data could be represented graphically as a flow diagram that shows the location of tasks or steps within a space and the flow of materials between tasks or steps. Figure 28 shows a flow diagram of the tasks listed in figure 27. You will need to refer to figure 27 to understand figure 28.

Use a flow diagram to help you see if a person or group within the process is handling materials more than once. Look for discontinuous numbered steps in an area. This represents times when materials return to a previous location for further handling. The simplest, most efficient workflow generally involves handling materials only once at each step in a process.

FIGURE 27
Completed Example of Workform 13: Workflow Chart

A. Location and/or work unit: technical services

B. Task or activity: Receiving, cataloging, and processing new materials

C. Starting point of task or activity: finding packing slip

D. Steps in the Task or Activity	Operation*	Transport*	Approval*	Storage*
1. Receive materials on dock	●	▷	◇	☐
2. Move boxes to receiving area in TS	○	▶	◇	☐
3. Find and open packing slip	●	▷	◇	☐
4. Open boxes	●	▷	◇	☐
5. Inspect materials for damage	●	▷	◇	☐
6. Sort and place materials on book trucks	●	▷	◇	☐
7. Count materials and mark packing slip	●	▷	◇	☐
8. Deliver materials and packing slip to acquisitions for check-in	○	▶	◇	☐
9. Receive materials in online system	●	▷	◇	☐
10. Sort new titles from added copies	●	▷	◇	☐
11. Send added copies to processing	○	▶	◇	☐
12. Move book trucks with new titles to holding shelves	○	▶	◇	☐
13. Put copies 2 through *n* on shelves by title	○	▷	◇	■
14. Send first copy of new titles to cataloging	○	▶	◇	☐
15. Search OCLC for cataloging copy	●	▷	◇	☐
16. Catalog titles found on OCLC	●	▷	◇	☐
17. Send completed copy cataloging titles to holding shelves to be matched with additional copies	○	▶	◇	☐
18. Send titles not in OCLC to original cataloger	○	▶	◇	☐
19. Catalog original titles in OCLC	●	▷	◇	☐
20. Review original cataloging for errors	○	▷	◆	☐
21. Send completed original cataloging titles to holding shelves to be matched with additional copies	○	▶	◇	☐
22. Retrieve all copies of newly cataloged titles from shelves and send to processing	○	▶	◇	☐
23. Complete physical processing of all items	●	▷	◇	☐
24. Send completely processed materials to shelves	○	▶	◇	☐

E. End point of task or process: materials leave technical services

*Definitions:
○ *Operation*—a step of actively handling materials to create an output
▷ *Transport*—the movement of inputs from one place to another during an activity
◇ *Approval*—a stopping point at which no further activity takes place until approval is given
☐ *Storage*—setting inputs aside at the end of a step until some other step is completed

Based on Robert Damelio, *The Basics of Process Mapping* (New York: Quality Resources, 1996).

FIGURE 28
Flow Diagram of Task or Step Sequences

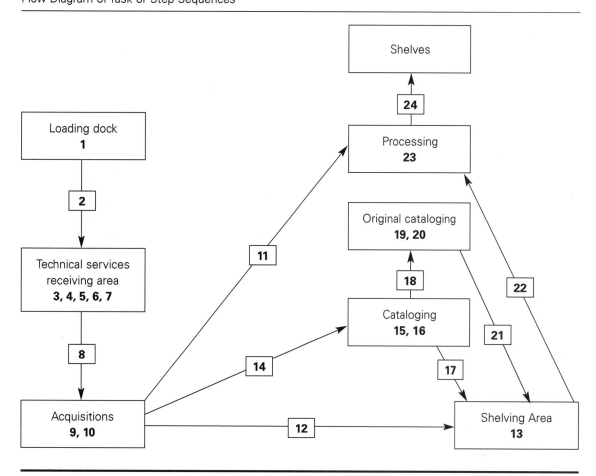

Based on Robert Damelio, *The Basics of Process Mapping* (New York: Quality Resources, 1996).

Another graphical way to represent the flow of a process through an area is to map it onto a floor plan of the location in which the work is done. Figure 29 maps the steps in the workflow chart from figure 27 to the floor plan of the technical services department.

Notice that the combination of the floor plan with the flow diagram gives you a much better picture of the movement of materials through the department. Can you see from figure 29 any changes in the organization of the department that might improve the flow of materials? Moving the storage bookshelves closer to acquisitions would reduce cross-room traffic, for example.

Another type of mapping used in process analysis is the classic flowchart. Flowcharts show the inputs, the sequence of steps, the decision points, and the outputs of an activity. Developing a flowchart, particularly if it is done as a group exercise with the staff that does the work, is an excellent way to understand how and why people do

FIGURE 29
Flow Diagram of Technical Services Department

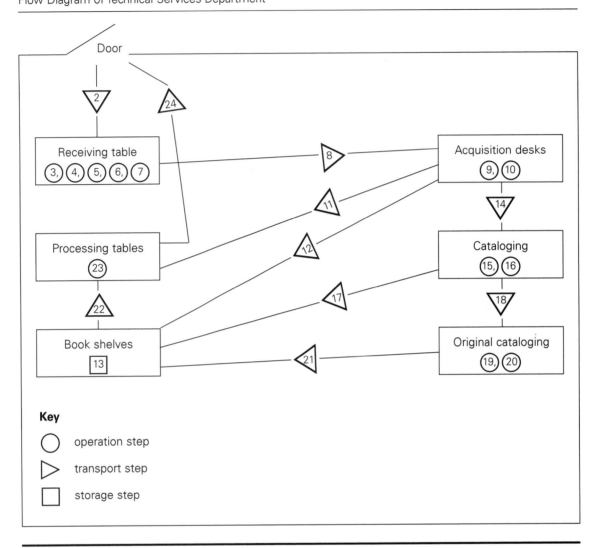

Based on Robert Damelio, *The Basics of Process Mapping* (New York: Quality Resources, 1996).

things. Often the act of developing the flowchart itself becomes the most powerful motivator for change. The discussions that go on as the flowchart is drawn can lead to immediate changes and improved working relationships among work groups and departments.

Many books are written on the process of flowcharting. Two of the most easily understood introductions are Dianne Galloway's *Mapping Work Processes* and *The Basics of Process Mapping* by Robert Damelio.[1]

As you saw in chapters 3 and 4, often the process of collecting data or filling out workforms allows you to see patterns, trends, and discrepancies that you hadn't seen before. These additional analytical techniques of gathering, arraying, and graphically presenting the data you've collected can help you see patterns and draw conclusions you literally hadn't seen before. Many times what had seemed to be an impenetrable problem starts to untangle once you write it down, create a chart from the data, or draw a process or flowchart on paper.

NOTE

1. Dianne Galloway, *Mapping Work Processes* (Milwaukee: ASQC Quality Press, 1994); Robert Damelio, *The Basics of Process Mapping* (New York: Quality Resources, 1996).

Chapter 6

Act on What You Learn

MILESTONES

By the time you finish this chapter you will know how to

- communicate the results of the project
- tailor the message on results and planned changes for each audience
- deal with staff resistance to change
- implement changes based on your results
- evaluate the effects of the changes
- integrate workload analysis into ongoing operations in the library

The reason for measuring workloads, setting baselines, and analyzing processes and the information your data-gathering efforts have produced is to make changes. These changes may involve

doing things differently

doing different things

understanding more thoroughly what work you do and the steps involved in doing this work

making work easier, smoother, or better for your staff

Change involves *action*. Someone must *do* something. These changes are probably going to involve more than the person who did the study and more than one person.

Communicating the Results

The people who have been immersed in any challenging project are often so tired and so close to the process that they forget that others don't know as much about it as they do. Even if you originally informed staff about the workload analysis project, you'll need to remind them of it and let them know that it's been completed. Make sure everyone knows what you learned and what the next steps will be in terms of implementation. If you haven't yet communicated widely about the project, do so now. Be sure to take the time to provide a context for the project and explain the purpose it was designed to serve.

You will have a variety of audiences for this information. The staff who were immediately affected by the project (that is, those who were studied or who helped with the study) and the staff in general are two audiences that need to hear about the project, the findings, and what will happen next as a result of the data gathering and analysis. The advisory group that helped plan and implement the project should be very much involved in developing the next steps based upon the results of the project, and they can be very effective in helping communicate this information.

Other audiences might include the leadership of the union that represents library staff members, your city or county manager, your library board, or your governing officials. Depending upon the situation that generated the study in the first place, the Friends, your foundation, the state library agency, or the media might be interested in your findings and implementation plans.

Just as you had to plan the project in the first place, you now have to plan the communication about what you learned and what you plan to do with that information. Identify the different audiences you need to reach, and consider how you should time your communications with them. Can you communicate with them simultaneously? If you can't, how can you manage the communications timetable so that feelings aren't hurt and political toes aren't stepped on? No one wants to read in the paper that his or her job is being changed or eliminated. The library assistants in technical services don't want to hear from their friends in circulation that processes they've been responsible for are going to be eliminated. Orchestrating the timing of these communications can be a challenge. Not paying attention to them will cause problems that will take much more time and attention in the long run than being sensitive and careful does in the short run.

Making Your Case

Because the end result of workload analysis is to make one or more changes, and because making these changes will likely involve a variety of people, your communications need to be not only informative but also persuasive. You need to persuade others to care about the situation that caused you to undertake the workload study initially, to accept the validity of your data, to agree with the analysis you've made of that data, and to concur with your assessment of what should be done to make the desired changes. This is a tall order. Thinking through what it is you want to accomplish will help you craft the most successful communications to your various audiences.

The first—and most important—step is to determine what it is you want the members of each specific audience to do. Then, think about what you can do to help them do that easily and quickly. You may want the general staff to know about the project, the results, and what will happen next and to believe that the project was conducted in a logical, fair way. If you've decided to eliminate date due slips in each book based on a study of circulation and processing procedures as a means to both reduce workers' compensation claims for repetitive motion injuries and to move materials through both areas more quickly, let staff know that was the purpose of the study. Give them a brief but quantitative picture of the study and the conclusions you have drawn from it. For example, point out that 14 million motions can be eliminated in the circulation department and 150,000 in the processing section, that two days were spent observing the processes and ten clerks filled out activity workforms, and that an analysis of workers' comp claims showed a 300 percent increase in claims over the last five years in these two work areas, etc. Tell them that circulation and processing staff members were involved in gathering and interpreting the data and explain what will happen next. For example, beginning October 1 date due slips will no longer be placed in books. Most importantly, let them know how they will be helped in implementing this new procedure. For example, circulation clerks will be given sample explanations they can give to the public, public relations materials will be prepared to inform library users of the change and the reasons for it, receipt printers will be in place, refrigerator magnets will be created as handouts to give the public.

This is a lot of information, but a change such as the preceding example will have an impact on all public service staff. Even the director's secretary needs to know about it, since he may get calls from library users who don't like the change or suspect that it's a ploy to generate additional fines.

The city manager, on the other hand, will want only a very distilled version of this communication. Succinct bulleted points describing the change and the reasons for the change, along with the assurance that knowledgeable staff were involved in the workload analysis project, should suffice. If you think there might be complaints, be sure to notify your superior and the appropriate boards before any problems arise. Assuring them that they have basic background information so they won't be surprised by possible public reaction will help smooth the way to a successful implementation.

A basic rule of thumb is that the higher in level or status the people you want to communicate with are, the less time and patience they have to focus on your communication. They want you to cut to the chase: state your proposal, the reasons for it (briefly!), and how much it will cost (usually in terms of money, but possibly in terms of people, time, or other resources). Everyone is busy and overloaded with information today. Learning how to convey the information that the receiver needs with sufficient but not extraneous explanation is a skill worth developing. Too often staff members and managers react to this feeling of being overloaded by saying that they don't want more communication. That really isn't what they mean, which you will find out the minute you don't communicate about something that affects them. Defining your audiences and identifying what you want them to do are techniques that will help you in crafting communications that will work for you and for those with whom you're trying to communicate.

Tailoring Your Presentation

Presenting information about the project and its results and what you're going to do next may take a number of forms. Consciously select the format of presentation based on the identified audiences and what you want them to do. Presentation options include

narratives These may be reports, articles, or other written documents that can be short, medium length, or long. You need to "tell your story" through a narrative logic that takes your audience along so that they reach the conclusion you desire.

tables, charts, graphs, and spreadsheets Such presentations may be part of a narrative document, or they may stand alone. These are usually the most effective ways to organize and present numerical and quantitative data. Experiment by trying different kinds of charts and graphs to see which format seems the most compelling to you. A picture often does convey a point much more effectively than a narrative description.

maps   A map provides a way to link information with spatial data. Maps can be floor plans overlaid with process flow data, or they can be geographic, providing a view of workload data linked to physical locations of your facilities. With the advent of desktop mapping software and GIS (Geographic Information System) programs, libraries, their parent jurisdictions, and vendors who specialize in providing this sort of documentation can create maps that show relationships among branch locations, usage intensity, and other factors.

process, workflow, and process improvement diagrams   Diagrams of this nature provide a way to visualize and analyze processes and the movement of work and materials. You may have used such tools in your data gathering and analysis. They may be useful to share with others to document your conclusions and recommendations. Highlighting important junctures or points with color, arrows, etc., can make these charts more persuasive in illustrating the bases for your conclusions.

Bev Bingham of the Tree County Public Library needs to make her case for technical services changes to two audiences: the director and the public services staff. Each presentation is tailored to the information needs of the target audience.

CASE STUDY

TREE COUNTY PUBLIC LIBRARY TECHNICAL SERVICES

Armed with her discoveries and her data, Bev talks with the director about making changes in the way Tree County catalogs nonprint media. She proposes that catalogers not view videos and DVDs if records are found on the library's bibliographic utility, even though this may occasionally result in less-than-complete cataloging records. The director says that Bev must gain the agreement of the public services staff before this policy change can be approved.

Bev makes a presentation to the senior management team, including the heads of all of the public services divisions. She presents the problem using results of the staff's numeric and process analyses and explains how the backlog grew. She then reminds the staff that the library's objective with the increased nonprint funding is to boost the availability and circulation of popular materials, not to build in-depth, permanent collections. Finally, she uses her projections, based on the changes proposed, to show how quickly technical services estimates the backlog can be made to disappear if the new changes are adopted.

After some discussion about the shelf life of nonprint materials (short compared to print), the collection development strategy for nonprint (popular, not scholarly, materials), and the public relations benefits of having popular titles available soon after publication, the staff agrees to Bev's proposed changes. It is decided that the changes will have little or no noticeable impact on staff or the public's ability to find these materials, so a brief memo to all staff saying that technical services is instituting changes that will speed up the delivery of new materials is all that is sent. Technical services staff, who had already been briefed on Bev's discussion with the director, begin to make the changes. At the end of the first month in which the changes were incorporated, the staff members celebrate the noticeable decrease in the size of the backlog.

Obtaining Approvals

It is possible that some sort of formal approval will be required before you implement the changes identified as a result of your workload analysis project. The need for outside approval will depend on the project, the reasons it was undertaken, the scope of the changes to be made, and the organizational structure of the library. If you are recommending changes in charges or fees, for example, the library board or the city council may have to give its approval because of the revenue implications. If you are changing the way work is done or the classification of the employees who do the work, you may have to negotiate or renegotiate a union agreement or at least meet notification requirements; on the other hand, you may have to rewrite job descriptions, which may involve human resources, the union, and the affected employees.

The ultimate communication may be a project report with recommendations that some person or group needs to approve. Once these approvals are secured (or modified recommendations are approved), implementation can begin.

Dealing with Change and Resistance

Depending upon the purpose of the workload analysis project, the data gathered from the project and the decisions made with this data are likely to involve change. This change could be about who does what, what is done, how it's done, or where it's done. Even if the data is used to staff a new building, the introduction of the new building into the library system will change the internal dynamics of the system and the way service is provided to users.

People adapt to change in a variety of ways and at various paces. Some on staff will be ready for it and eager to adopt the new methodologies, assignments, and arrangements. Others will be slower to accept it but will come around once they have more information about how the change will affect them and their work lives. Some will get on board even later, and some may never adopt the change.

Scores of books and training sessions have been produced on change and change management. Most experts on the topic agree that there are six major reasons for resistance:[1]

1. *Perceived negative outcome*   The people or group impacted think that they will be negatively affected.

2. *Fear of more work*   People fear that the result will be more work for them without additional compensation or support from others.

3. *Habits must be broken*   People's work habits are an interrelated combination of behaviors. Changing even one can cause a domino effect of other changes that may be even harder to accommodate.

4. *Lack of communication*   It's virtually impossible for an organization to overcommunicate. People need to hear, in a variety of ways, what is going to happen, why, to whom, by whom, when, etc. What may be crystal clear to the library director or the manager implementing the workload analysis project may not be in the employees' zone of awareness until they see that it really does affect them.

5. *Failure to align with the organization as a whole*   Organizations are complex systems. Successful change requires support from and integration with the library's structure, business systems, technology, core competencies, employee knowledge, and skills and culture (values, norms, beliefs, and assumptions). Ensuring this alignment is a major undertaking itself.

6. *Employee rebellion*   People often don't resist the change itself, but they do resist having it forced upon them without sufficient acknowledgment of the many implications it can have. Being forced to accept change means you've lost control of your work life. Very few people are comfortable with losing control, especially in a profession as organized and rule-driven as library service.

Don't expect to avoid resistance. We all resist that which we think will harm us or the people or things (like our definition of good customer service) that are important to us. Be prepared for it, and learn from it. Strong reactions or emotions are indicative of deeper issues that need to be addressed. Resistance gives you valuable information about the situation:

> how things used to be and why
>
> implications you didn't think of
>
> blind spots in your own thinking and about the person who is resistant
>
> hints about where an individual's thinking is stuck (misinformation?, late adopter?, etc.)

Managing change effectively is a challenging, ongoing responsibility. Whether the contemplated change is large or small, following are some key points to keep in mind:[2]

> *Establish the need to change.*   People need to not only know why you think it's important to change something but to accept that

need themselves so they actually will make the change. Usually this requires a crisis level of intensity or urgency. Why should people bother to change the way they do *their* work unless there is a compelling reason that will affect *them*? The reason you provide has to be accompanied by a vision that really grabs them of how things will be better.

Create a clear, compelling vision that shows people how their lives will be better. It really does come down to "what's in it for me?"—and that makes sense. If people don't understand how the proposed change will have an impact on them and what they do in the library, and if that change doesn't seem to make sense within their larger sense of things, the proposal will be met with skepticism and disaffection.

Show true performance improvements early on. Except for those rare few who embrace change early and enthusiastically, most employees want to see the proof of the effectiveness of the new way of doing things. Seeing this will motivate them to become change advocates and should result in more improvements. Library employees take a pragmatic approach and will react positively to positive results. The trick is to be sure that everyone's definition of success is the same, which goes back to the initial project purpose and outcome definitions.

Communicate, communicate, communicate. Most change efforts that fail do so primarily because of inadequate and ineffective communication. Two strata of communication will be necessary for the workload analysis project: the larger purpose/vision about why the project is being undertaken and the actual details of what is being done, who is doing it, the timetable, results gathered, and the actions to be taken based on these results.

Build a sponsoring team to manage the change process that includes top management. In many libraries, the director or a senior manager will be in charge of the workload analysis project and the implementation of the changes. In larger, more-complex library systems, the project may be initiated and implemented by a middle manager or lower-level supervisor or a work group. Whatever the structure, it's important that the library as a whole and those who will be most affected by the change know that there is administrative support for the changes to be made. If the proposed changes are meeting significant resistance or seem markedly disruptive, it is even more important that the director's support is reaffirmed and conveyed throughout the organization.

Don't fear complexity. Some organizational change specialists counsel that organizations should make wide, sweeping changes rather than incremental changes and that these broader change efforts will actually be easier in the long run. The most appropriate use of this point in relationship to workload analysis efforts is that what may seem like a minor adjustment to a work process or work assignment can often have repercussions that go far beyond one work area. For example, many libraries have decided to eliminate date due slips in books. The decision makes sense in terms of workload and work environment. However, this simple change often results in a firestorm of library customer reaction that then results in circulation clerks and others advocating for the retention of the date due slip and forgetting why the change was made in the first place.

Recognize that it is easier for people to support their own ideas. Involving people in the change process, from the beginning step of conceptualizing the project through analyzing the data and making decisions based on the data, is an essential ingredient in acquiring support for the ultimate changes. The library employees involved in the project develop their understanding of the processes involved and the changes to be made. Involving them in the communications activities enhances the effectiveness of the process and the acceptance of the final results.

Negotiation

Disagreements about the proposed changes, even second-guessing the project itself, are bound to arise. People will have different perspectives, different experiences and mental models, and different reactions to the results based on the culture and climate of the library and their own values and priorities. These differences will have to be negotiated with staff to achieve agreement. Too often managers and project leaders rely upon logic and reason as their only negotiation tool. This will rarely be sufficient.

Jeff Crow provides a helpful way to look at the issues around which most negotiations revolve:

facts

goals

methods

values[3]

Issues of fact are the easiest issues to resolve because they can be verified. There may need to be discussion about the methodology of deriving them, but after that the facts should lead to acceptance. Last year's circulation figures for the Ash and the Pine branches, for example, are facts.

Goals can be more difficult to come to agreement on. For example, is the goal to increase circulation at Maple Branch? Perhaps that goal doesn't make sense to some staff and the branch manager because Maple's lower socioeconomic population uses the library as a community center and as a place to read and study but not so much as a place to borrow books.

Agreement gets much trickier around methodology. There may be a number of ideas on how to implement changes, with different costs and considerations for each one. There will be different probabilities of success and much speculation about methods that haven't been tried (or were tried and rejected before).

Can values be negotiated? Some say they are so personal that they can't be. If the issue seems to be one of values, that identification is important, and the project manager should proceed with caution. Can he or she work to define the values more specifically? Maybe the group can agree that providing good customer service is a widely held value and agree that there can be differences in how that value is defined and accomplished. This is the point where negotiation skills will be extremely valuable.

What are the basic skills of negotiation? One of the best books on the subject provides extensive amplification of these basic tactics:[4]

Create a common ground. Establish what you already agree on. In your workload analysis project, the library director, the project manager, and the advisory group (if there was one) agreed on a project goal, for example, that the new, larger building should have adequate staffing to give service at least at the same level as the existing building.

Enlarge areas of agreement. Build and enlarge upon that on which you already agree and have in common as an interest. Work with others to find alternatives that meet both your needs and theirs. Your children's librarian might balk at the idea of using paraprofessionals to provide services to children. It may be more palatable to her if she gets agreement that she will continue to select books, oversee the library assistant, and be freed up to make visits to local schools, which actually expands services.

Gather information. Find out the details of concerns or problems. Know who is concerned and the specifics of their concern. In libraries, problems are often presented by one employee on behalf of another or are based on incomplete information. Work to get to the bottom of the situation. There may be verifiable facts that can be dealt with. For example, perhaps the union steward has told you that the circulation clerks at Elm Branch say the self-checkout machine in their branch doesn't work and that expanding the self-checkout program will be a mistake. Is the machine malfunctioning? Is it in the right location to attract users? Are the clerks afraid that the machine will ultimately take their jobs or their hours away? Is the problem that the machine works but won't accept videos because they have to be handled differently? There are a lot of facts and assumptions and fears to unearth and address.

Focus on issues, not personalities   One of the basic tenets of effective negotiation is to avoid getting hooked by someone else's emotions or approaches. It's important to understand the human dimension of any interaction but to operate at the next level rather than reacting to provocative statements or behaviors. Say: "What are we going to do about this?" rather than "Why did you let us get into this mess?"

All of the challenges described here may leave you thinking that nothing you will learn is worth the trials you will face in acting on the information. It is true that the first workload project you undertake is likely to be challenging if your staff has never participated in a workload analysis project. However, a well-designed effort that involves staff and respects their input and contributions can pay unforeseen dividends. Listening to staff and working *with* them to make their work more productive or less tedious, or to create and recognize a more direct relationship between their effort and the objectives of the library, can create a new culture within your organization. As staff members learn to trust that you are not using workload analysis as a punitive tool but are truly committed to improving service and eliminating tasks that don't contribute to achieving objectives, you may find, as many libraries have, that staff can be your best allies in these efforts.

Let's look at some of the results from the Tree County Public Library reference workload analysis.

CASE STUDY

TREE COUNTY PUBLIC LIBRARY REFERENCE SERVICES

The advisory group working on the reference workload project eagerly analyzes the observation workforms. They are excited because for the first time everyone's impressions and own personal reactions to stress are being complemented by actual data. At Birch and Maple 25 percent of reference desk tasks involve PCs, compared with 5 percent at the other branches. The observers noted that many of the PC users at Birch are children from the nearby school and that Maple has a number of elderly PC users, especially in the mornings at the same time as school visits and preschool story hours. The observers also note that the printer at Maple is frequently broken, which means there are more problems and patron interactions.

Because work involving PCs is a big part of desk work at Birch and Maple, and because security interactions are significant in those two branches as well as at Elm, the group decides to gather one more set of data. Staff will use Workforms 9 and 11 to more thoroughly define and analyze the tasks and steps involved in providing PC assistance and interacting with problem patrons or dealing with security issues. Just talking about these two issues reveals a number of additional findings:

No one really understands how to report or track security issues, so there is no baseline data.

The printer model selected for the branches can't take the heavy demand placed on it.

There is no backup equipment ready to be used when something breaks down.

Many of the PC users are children who need a combination of instruction, assistance with homework, and just plain attention after school.

In addition, two afternoons a week the Birch Branch children's librarian is out of the branch, telling stories at a local hospital.

When the workforms come back, everyone sees that the security incidents and the heavy PC usage are clumped in the same branches and at the same times. "I never thought I'd be the one to suggest volunteers," Myra offered, "but it seems to me it would help us if we got people to just be out on the floor to assist people with the basics and with the routine things like paper jams, scheduling the PCs, and so on. I know that the senior center has a group of trainers who might be perfect for the seniors at Maple. Maybe they could help out after school, too. It wouldn't be that hard to train them to know when to refer people to us."

The group decides to seek approval to pursue this idea and to begin looking at other ideas that seem to make sense based on their findings. They decide to send a report out to all the reference staff, asking for volunteers to serve on a committee they call "reexamining reference desk services."

Zeke agrees to brief the library director on their findings and to get her blessing for the new committee and the volunteers. He also talks with the head of Birch Branch about service priorities for the children's librarian. He can already feel some of the tension dissipating now that the staff can take some positive steps to address the issues they have uncovered.

Implementation

The end of your workload analysis project will probably mean the beginning of work for others as you move from considering change to implementing change. While a detailed explanation of implementation steps is beyond the scope of this book, it is important to keep several points in mind because too often people forget that there are many details that need to be dealt with beyond communicating the results of the project. These details include

developing new policies and procedures and documenting them

ordering supplies or equipment needed to implement the change

developing and delivering necessary training

developing and distributing public relations materials designed to explain the changes to the library's users

updating existing brochures, Web sites, and other materials to reflect the changes

communicating changes to institutional or community partners, as necessary

negotiating changes in labor union contracts, personnel rules, work rules, etc., as necessary

negotiating changes with outside vendors and service providers, as necessary

When and How

When can all of the details listed previously be done? Should implementation coincide with a larger event such as the beginning of the calendar year, the fiscal year, or the school year? Will needed personnel be available at the time you want to implement changes? Is the time line contingent upon others completing activities (hiring, contract review, etc.) that will affect implementation? Consider all the timing issues.

What will the consequences of implementing these changes be on other processes and activities? Even minor changes can send ripples through an organization. You can prepare for undesirable impacts by contemplating the ramifications of the proposed changes and the impact implementation of them will have on the whole organization. Such consideration is a key part of systems thinking.[5]

Staged Implementation

Your consideration of the impact and timing of changes may cause you to conclude that you can't implement all the changes or you can't implement them all at the same time throughout your library system. You have two options: You can develop one or several pilot implementation locations, or you can institute a rolling, or staged, implementation. Pilot projects allow you to try out the changes in one or several locations to see if they produce the anticipated results and to test procedures, fine-tune training requirements, reveal communications issues, and so on. A pilot project allows you and staff to practice in a more controlled environment than a systemwide implementation provides. It also should involve an evaluation before the final decision is made to reproduce the implementation elsewhere in the system.

Rolling or staged implementations allow you to break down implementation into more manageable chunks. You might decide to implement a change by size of library, geographic area, time period (such as three a quarter, five each year, or once a month), or some other criteria (such as branches that serve the most children, are located near schools, serve a large number of Spanish-speaking people, or are reopening after renovation). This implementation approach implicitly means that the changes will be made; however, the changes are being made in a managed way or are triggered by some criteria.

Success Factors or Indicators

How will you know if the changes you made "worked"? You had something in mind when you started the workload analysis project. Be sure to articulate once again what you were trying to accomplish and determine what the measurement of that accomplishment will be. This may be a target (each circulation clerk handles an average of 50,000 checkouts per year), an efficiency goal (technical services will handle a materials budget increase of 20 percent without adding permanent staff members), an effectiveness goal (patrons will receive the high demand items they've requested within three weeks of their request), or an improvement goal (the number of steps involved in paying an invoice will be reduced by 30 percent).

Include indicators of public and staff satisfaction, also. Be prepared to assess fairly the impact the changes have had. Decide what period of time is reasonable for staff and the public to get accustomed to the changes. Don't decide that the change didn't work if you receive some complaints during the first few weeks. On the other hand, if you receive dozens of complaints weekly after six months, there may be something wrong with the change or with how it was implemented or explained. Now is the time to establish some baselines for feedback, if you don't already have them. Do you know what level of feedback you usually get? Can you tell if you're getting "a lot" or only a few complaints?

Staff and public feedback can also be invaluable in planning future workload projects. All of the services libraries provide are based on work that library staffs perform. The process of developing and analyzing services is an ongoing one. What you learn from this project can and should be applied to the next one.

Remember that change is incremental. Change isn't easy. It takes a lot of effort and a lot of work and often a change in attitudes and a reconsideration of values. What seems logical to you may not seem that way to others. What seems like irrefutable evidence to you based on the data you've collected may not outweigh perceptions of service requirements and necessities by others. If this is the first time you've collected data, analyzed processes, and applied analytical techniques in your library, others may feel uncomfortable with this approach. You need to retain your confidence in these techniques while accepting that progress is often a matter of taking two steps forward and one step back.

Celebrate

Don't forget the importance of celebrating the last step in your workload analysis project. Find fun, interesting, creative ways to celebrate the completion of the project; the elimination of outdated, needless, just plain silly steps in procedures and work processes; and the discovery of ways to make the work less tedious, more responsive, and more fulfilling. Everyone involved in the project has worked hard. Acknowledge the hard work and support of the staff involved, the advisory group, and others who have contributed. Acknowledge the hard spots, and reinforce the insights and willingness to change that staff and managers have demonstrated. If there are some areas that have been left unresolved, acknowledge those too, and let people know what will happen next so they are not left hanging. How you manage the end of the project can be as important in determining the project's success as any other step.

Some libraries celebrate the completion of a project by sharing the project process and findings (as well as the cake) with others on staff. Some management teams treat the other staff members as a way of saying "thank you" and "well done." Sometimes work groups have open houses in their work area to demonstrate the changes they've made as a result of the project to other staff members, governing officials, or library board members. These events all are ways of recognizing the hard work and creativity of the staff members involved and of marking the beginning of the implementation of the changes that are to be made.

The Cycle of Improvement

The types of questions that prompted you to read this book and undertake a workload project never go away. Workload analysis is a tool that you will use on an ongoing basis. The completion of one analysis may well kick off the commencement of the next. Each cycle involves more questions being raised, more interesting data being discovered, and an evaluation of the implementation activities and outcomes.

The plan-do-check-act cycle (sometimes referred to as the Shewhart Cycle or the Deming Cycle) is another essential tool in the total quality management toolbox. (See figure 30.) It was designed as a way to apply the scientific method to improving quality in organizations. The changes that come out of workload analysis are definitely quality improvements. The cycle starts at the top and moves around the circle clockwise.

Plan is the part of the process you've just completed with your workload analysis project: identification and definition of the problem, data gathering and analysis, recommendations for change, and development of the implementation plan.

Do involves communicating the implementation plan, carrying out the plan, and gathering data about how the implementation went.

Check is the evaluation step. Using the techniques explained in this book, take a look at how things went.

Act involves making changes and adjustments, fine-tuning the implementation plan, and making changes so that what had been an implementation plan becomes an institutionalized, accepted practice of doing things. The cycle then starts again as what is new becomes stale and ultimately has to be examined once again.

The cycle isn't one cycle but a series of cycles, moving you forward along a course of never-ending improvement. The iterative nature of

FIGURE 30

Plan, Do, Check, Act Cycle

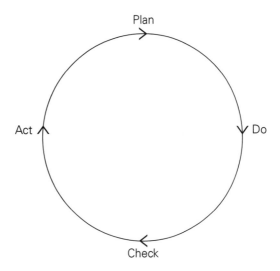

this process may seem daunting as you complete the first cycle. Remember that you've learned a lot and your staff have also. You are now familiar with the tools and techniques and have gained experience in using them. When faced with questions of how many staff you need, whether your operations are as efficient as they can be, or how best to absorb budget cuts, you have the tools you need to make reasonable decisions based on data.

NOTES

1. Joseph H. Boyett and Jimmie T. Boyett, *The Guru Guide: The Best Ideas of the Top Management Thinkers* (New York: John Wiley, 1998), 49–56.

2. Ibid., 57–78.

3. Jeff Crow, *Applying Project Management* (Portland, Ore.: Blackbird, 1999), 3-29–35.

4. Roger Fisher, Willam Ury, and Bruce Patton, *Getting to Yes: Negotiating Agreement without Giving in.* 2d ed. (New York: Penguin, 1991).

5. Systems thinking involves thinking of the organization as a whole, understanding that its elements continually affect each other, and recognizing that these patterns of interrelationship flow, loop, and influence each other. A good overview of the concept is provided in Peter M. Senge and others, *The Fifth Discipline Fieldbook: Strategies and Tools for Building a Learning Organization* (New York: Doubleday, 1994), 87–190.

Instructions and Workforms

1   Workload Analysis Project Overview   112

2   Estimate of Productive Work Hours Available   117

3   Determining Who Does What   120

4   Standard Terms in Our Library for Tasks and Steps   122

General Instructions for Analysis of Staff Time   126
  5   Analysis of Staff Time: Work Unit Estimate of Time Spent on Activities   127

6   Analysis of Staff Time: Individual Estimate of Time Spent on Activities   129

General Instructions for Recording Staff Tasks   131
  7   Recording Staff Tasks: Self-Report Log   132

8   Recording Staff Tasks: Direct Observation Log   135

General Instructions for Analysis of a Task   139
  9   Analysis of a Task:
      Observation   140
      Self-Report   142

10   Time Spent on an Input-Driven Task   145

11   Time Spent on a Demand-Driven Task   148

12   Time Spent on Public Desks   151

13   Workflow Chart   154

WORKFORM 1   Workload Analysis Project Overview

Instructions

Purpose of Workform 1

Use this workform to organize your workload analysis project.

Who Should Complete Workform 1?

The manager of the workload analysis project will fill out the workform.

Sources of Data for Workform 1

The project manager, advisory group, and others involved in the planning of the project will provide the data for this workform.

Factors to Consider When Completing Workform 1

Identifying the project goal and envisioning what a successful project will look like at the end are key elements in planning a workload analysis project. They are crucial to determining when you have gathered enough data to make your decision.

To Complete Workform 1

Answer each question on the workform. Do not begin the project until you have answers for each question.

Factors to Consider When Reviewing Workform 1

1. Are there sufficient resources, especially staff time, to complete the project on schedule?

2. Have you involved the key stakeholders in your plan?

WORKFORM 1 Workload Analysis Project Overview

A. Project Definition

1. What is the goal of this study? What do you want to accomplish?

_____

_____

_____

2. What will a successful project look like at the end? What changes might result from this study?

_____

_____

_____

B. Data Gathering

1. What do you need to know? What factors affect the project goal?

_____

_____

_____

2. What data do you currently collect on the factors that affect the goal?

_____

_____

_____

(Continued)

113

3. Analyze the data you already have. Does the data provide enough information for you to make a decision that achieves the project goal? If so, write your results and decision below and STOP the project.

_____

_____

_____

4. If you need more data, what data do you need? Do you need to know:

• Who does the work?

• How it is done?

• How long will a task or the steps in the task take?

• How many outputs are produced?

_____

_____

_____

_____

5. Does the data need to be precise, or will estimates do?

_____

(Continued)

6. How will you gather the data? Which workforms will you use?

_____

_____

_____

7. Who will complete the workforms? Who will train the people who will complete the workforms?

_____

_____

_____

8. What is the time line for completing the workforms? Who will supervise the data-gathering effort?

_____

_____

_____

9. What is the time line for completing the project?

_____

_____

_____

(Continued)

C. Results

1. Who will analyze the data and develop the results?

    _____

2. Who will determine if the project goal is met or if additional data might change the decision?

    _____

D. Communication

1. Who should be told about the project before it begins? As it is underway? After the results are developed?

    _____

    _____

    _____

    _____

2. What communications strategies will you use for each audience at each stage?

    _____

    _____

    _____

    _____

Completed by _____   Date completed _____

Source of data _____   Library _____

Purpose of Workform 2

Use this workform to calculate the total number of hours available annually for any one category of staff.

Sources of Data for Workform 2

The library personnel policy and the library budget for staff provide the information for this workform.

Factors to Consider When Completing Workform 2

1. Complete a copy of this workform for each staff category shown at the top of the workform.

2. Part of the workform focuses on predictable and unpredictable time away from work. Both kinds of time are authorized, but predictable time is routine, while the unpredictable time varies by circumstances affecting staff.

3. Be sure to account for differences in vacation days authorized for seniority among staff in the same category.

4. You might want to compile a summary sheet to calculate the total work hours available for any unit/team.

5. Do not enter data in the shaded sections.

To Complete Workform 2

An example of a completed workform is provided as a guide to assist you in completing this workform.

1. **Lines A–D** Complete the information at the top of the workform.

    Line A Record the number of full-time staff in a job category.

    Line B Record the name of the unit/team in which these staff work.

    Line C Record the total number of staff eligible for benefits. Then divide this number into two groups—those eligible for standard vacation and those eligible for seniority vacation.

Line D Record the number of hours in the standard work week for full-time staff in this job classification.

2. **Lines E–F** Calculate the nominal staff hours per year by multiplying line A × line D × 52 weeks. (See the worked example of Workform 2.) Record the answer in the unshaded area of row F.

3. **Section G** Calculate the number of predictable hours unavailable by multiplying the times authorized for vacation, holidays, and work breaks by the number of staff eligible in this job category. Record the number of hours for each in the unshaded section for each row.

    Row G5 Add all the hours in section G and record the total in the unshaded section for the row.

4. **Section H** Record all time taken as sick or personal leave by this staff category last year. For an indication of the worst-case estimate, record all total hours for sick leave, personal days, and other (funeral time, jury duty, etc.) authorized.

    Row H4 Add the total number of hours used or authorized for sick leave, personal days, and other. Record the total in the unshaded section for the row.

5. **Row I** Add the numbers in rows G5 and H4 and record the total.

6. **Row J** Subtract row I from row F and enter the difference in row J.

7. **Row K** If you know the number of hours budgeted or authorized for part-time staff for the fiscal year, record that number in row K.

8. **Row L** Add rows J and K and record the total in row L.

Factors to Consider When Reviewing Workform 2

1. Remember that the figure for available hours is only an estimate.

2. The time worked by part-time staff needs to be included for a complete picture of a unit's available staff hours. Be sure to subtract the time these employees are on break each day.

3. If the library provides sick leave or vacation for part-time staff, use this workform to determine the number of part-time staff hours available.

WORKFORM 2　Estimate of Productive Work Hours Available—*Example*

A. Indicate the number and level of staff in **one** of the categories below.

Librarians _____　Library assistants __8__　Clerical _____　Pages _____

B. Unit/team ___Ash Branch___

C. Number of staff eligible for benefits __8__　for standard vacation __6__　for seniority vacation __2__

D. Hours in standard work week __40__

E. Nominal staff hours available per year: number of staff __8__ × hours in standard work week __40__ × 52 weeks/yr. = __16,640__

F. Nominal staff hours available/year				16,640
G. Predictable hours unavailable				
1. Vacation				
Standard vacation hours [80 at Ash] × number of staff eligible [6]	480			
Seniority vacation hours [80 at Ash] × number of staff eligible [2]	160			
2. Holidays (in hours)	640			
3. Daily customary breaks (2 × 15 min. × number staff)	960			
4. Other	0			
5. Total predictable hours unavailable		2,240		
H. Unpredictable hours unavailable				
1. Sick leave	192			
2. Personal days	128			
3. Other	40			
4. Total unpredictable hours unavailable			360	
I. Grand total hours unavailable				−2,600
J. Actual full-time staff hours available for year				14,040
K. Number hours of part-time staff budgeted this year				+1,000
L. Total hours available for this level per year				15,040

Completed by ___Art Arnold___　　Date completed ___10/15___

Source of data ___personnel records___　　Library ___Ash Branch___

WORKFORM 2   Estimate of Productive Work Hours Available

A. Indicate the number and level of staff in **one** of the categories below.

Librarians _____   Library assistants _____   Clerical _____   Pages _____

B. Unit/team _____

C. Number of staff eligible for benefits _____   for standard vacation _____   for seniority vacation _____

D. Hours in standard work week _____

E. Nominal staff hours available per year: number staff _____ × hours in standard work week _____ × 52 weeks/yr. = _____

F. Nominal staff hours available/year			
G. Predictable hours unavailable			
1. Vacation			
Standard vacation hours × number of staff eligible			
Seniority vacation hours × number of staff eligible			
2. Holidays (in hours)			
3. Daily customary breaks (2 × 15 min. × number staff)			
4. Other			
5. Total predictable hours unavailable			
H. Unpredictable hours unavailable			
1. Sick leave			
2. Personal days			
3. Other			
4. Total unpredictable hours unavailable			
I. Grand total hours unavailable			
J. Actual full-time staff hours available for year			
K. Number hours of part-time staff budgeted this year			
L. Total hours available for this level per year			

Completed by _____   Date completed _____

Source of data _____   Library _____

WORKFORM 3   Determining Who Does What

Instructions

Purpose of Workform 3

Use this workform to collect information about who does what activities and tasks in a work location or work unit.

Who Should Complete Workform 3?

Supervisors or managers in the work area under review who are familiar with the tasks involved in the activity being studied should fill out the workform.

Source of Data for Workform 3

Create a list of the tasks in the activity being studied.

Factors to Consider When Completing Workform 3

1. The tasks listed can range from very general to quite specific, depending on the level of detail you need for your study. For example, aggregating tasks into a single collective task (i.e., "shelving books" rather than "presort books onto trucks, preread shelves and shift as needed, file returned materials on shelves") may supply the information you need. The more encompassing the task, the easier it is to collect data about that task. However, aggregated data is less precise and may obscure problem areas. Your results may indicate a need for further study that can be accomplished only at a more-detailed level. This workform may be used multiple times—at increasing levels of specificity—as you study your library's workloads.

2. The list of tasks can be derived from a brainstorming session among those most familiar with the tasks assigned to the locations or work units being studied. You may want to pretest the resulting list to be sure the list is inclusive and that terms used are familiar to those who will be completing the workform.

3. The workform may be completed using individual staff names or job classifications. Whichever choice you make, be consistent throughout the workform. If you intend to compare data across multiple work units, be consistent in your selection across the multiple work units.

   Using job classifications will make it easier for managers not directly involved in the work to analyze the results, since it will not require familiarity with individual staff to evaluate the data. Using job classifications also may be less threatening to individual staff, but it may not give you the level of specificity you require, especially in small work units.

   You may also have several staff in the same job classification within a work unit who do different work. If that is the case and you choose not to use personal names, you may want to append a letter or number (Library Technician A) to the job classification to distinguish among the individuals.

4. Job classifications responsible for tasks should be listed regardless of whether the person doing the work is full- or part-time.

5. If a volunteer is responsible for the task, that should be noted.

6. Both primary and secondary or backup responsibilities should be indicated as appropriate. Use *P* to indicate the person or position that has primary responsibility for performing this task most of the time. Use *S* (for secondary) to indicate the person or position that performs the task when the primary person is unavailable or cannot complete the task without assistance.

To Complete Workform 3

1. **Item A**   Write the location or work unit in which the activity is done.

2. **Item B**   Write the activity being studied.

3. **Column C**   List the major tasks associated with the activity, one per numbered line.

4. **Columns D**   Write the job classifications or the name of the staff member in the work unit on the line under each column D *heading*, one classification per column. Use additional copies of the workform if you need to include more than four columns for D.

   On each numbered line with an activity, write a *P* if the staff member or job classification listed under the heading in this column has primary responsibility for the activity. Write an *S* if the person or job listed in this column has backup or secondary responsibility for the activity.

Factors to Consider When Reviewing Workform 3

1. Are the same tasks being done by staff in different classifications either within or across the work units you are assessing? If so, should that continue?

2. Are the classifications of staff doing each task appropriate for that task?

3. Are the tasks that are being carried out appropriate to this work unit and consistent with library policy?

WORKFORM 3 Determining Who Does What

A. Location and/or work unit _____

B. Activity _____

C. Tasks	**D. Job Classification or Name:** ___	**D. Job Classification or Name:** ___	**D. Job Classification or Name:** ___	**D. Job Classification or Name:** ___
1.				
2.				
3.				
4.				
5.				
6.				
7.				
8.				
9.				
10.				
11.				
12.				
13.				
14.				
15.				

Completed by _____ Date completed _____

Source of data _____ Library _____

Purpose of Workform 4

Use this workform to provide staff with a standard set of terms they can use to complete the workload data-gathering workforms.

Who Should Complete Workform 4?

The project leaders for the workload analysis effort should complete this workform and distribute it with other workforms provided to staff to gather data for the project.

Sources of Data for Workform 4

1. Workforms 3 and 9 are sources of data for this workform. Deriving the terms you will use for tasks and steps from pretests of those workforms will ensure that the data you gather from multiple staff will be more easily compiled. Standardizing terms will also facilitate comparisons across locations and work units and between varying time periods.

2. The terms you choose to enter on Workform 4 will reflect your own organization's workflow and the needs of the specific study you are conducting. There is no universal definition of library tasks and steps that you can reference or use here.

Factors to Consider When Completing Workform 4

1. Keep these definitions in mind as you complete the workform:

   a *task* is a set of steps staff take to accomplish a measurable output

   a *step* is a discrete action taken in sequence in the performance of a task

2. The tasks and steps you list can range from very general to quite specific, depending on the level of detail you need for your study.

3. Aggregating multiple tasks or steps into a single listed task or step (i.e., "PC assistance" rather than "fix printer, help patron find information, manage sign-up sheets") may supply the information you need. The more encompassing the task or step is, the easier it is to collect data about it. Note that when you aggregate steps you may end up with tasks that have only one step. Samples of aggregated steps are included on the examples of the completed workform.

4. Be aware that aggregated data may obscure problem areas. Your results may indicate a need for further study that can only be accomplished at a more detailed

level. This workform may be used multiple times, at increasing levels of detail, as you study your library's workloads.

To Complete Workform 4

Examples of completed workforms are provided as a guide to assist you in completing this workform.

1. **Item A**   Write the term your library will use to describe this activity. Note that the activity might be very broad, (providing services at the circulation desk), or it might be narrow (returning materials to the shelves or processing new videotapes for shelving), depending on the level of specificity or detail you are studying.

2. **Item B**   Write a description of what is included in this activity.

3. **Item C**   Write the task you are studying if you are using this workform to record vocabulary for *steps in a task*. If you are recording vocabulary for tasks in an activity, you will leave this line blank.

4. **Column D**   Circle the word "tasks" if you are listing tasks here. Circle the word "steps" if you are listing steps here.

   Write the term your library will use to describe each task in this activity or step in this task. Note that you may aggregate multiple actions into one listed task or step because of the way the work flows, because of the difficulty of timing a particular action, or because you do not need a great deal of precision for the data you are gathering.

5. **Column E**   On each numbered line with a task or step, write a brief description of what is included in that task or step.

Factors to Consider When Reviewing Workform 4

1. Are the terms understandable to the staff who do the work you are measuring?

2. Is each task or step long enough to be usefully measured? Could a staff member or an observer identify the starting and stopping point of each task or step?

3. Is it clear what is included in each task or step? Can a staff member or observer distinguish among the listed tasks or steps which one is being performed at any point in time? Is there any overlap among the tasks or steps? If so, remove any duplication before providing these terms to staff to use when completing other workforms.

WORKFORM 4   **Standard Terms in Our Library for Tasks and Steps—*Example***

A. Activity: <u>Providing services at the information desk</u>

B. Description: <u>This activity includes answering reference and directional questions, searching for requested titles</u>
<u>and placing holds, collection management, and reader's advisory work.</u>

C. Task: _____

D. Tasks/Steps	**E. Definition**
1. Holds	Includes searching shelves for materials and placing holds for materials not found
2. Information service	Includes answering directional and reference questions and providing instruction on the OPAC and electronic databases
3. Collection management	Includes reading reviews, ordering materials, weeding the collection, and changing shelving locations in the OPAC as needed
4. Reader's advisory	Includes providing advice on reading selections
5.	
6.	
7.	
8.	

Completed by <u>Irene Inez</u>   Date completed <u>10/31</u>

Source of data <u>Workform 3</u>   Library <u>Maple Branch</u>

123

WORKFORM 4 Standard Terms in Our Library for Tasks and Steps—*Example*

A. Activity: Providing services at the circulation desk

B. Description: This activity includes giving patrons applications and entering patron data into the database, checking out materials, accepting fine payments, retrieving hold materials and calling patrons, and handling "claims returned" materials.

C. Task: Input patron information into database

D. Tasks/Steps	E. Definition
1. Code workform with statistical data	Includes determining age and geographic location categories
2. Search database for existing record and, if found, edit record	Includes entering search and assessing found records for match and changing bar code and other data as needed for found records
3. Enter patron data if no existing record is found	Includes entering all data from patron application workform
4.	
5.	
6.	
7.	
8.	

Completed by   Cindy Carver

Source of data   Workform 9

Date completed   10/31

Library   Maple Branch

WORKFORM 4 **Standard Terms in Our Library for Tasks and Steps**

A. Activity: _____

B. Description: _____
_____

C. Task: _____

D. Tasks/Steps	**E. Definition**
1.	
2.	
3.	
4.	
5.	
6.	
7.	
8.	

Completed by _____ Date completed _____

Source of data _____ Library _____

General Instructions

Purpose of Workforms 5–6

Use these workforms to identify the activities a staff member is assigned to and the amount of time each activity takes.

Who Should Complete Workforms 5–6?

Workform 5 should be completed by the supervisor of a work unit. Workform 6 should be completed by the staff members whose work is being studied.

Sources of Data for Workforms 5–6

1. Either self-reports from staff (Workform 6) or the estimates of the work unit supervisor (Workform 5) are the basis for this information.

2. Workform 4 can be used to develop common terms or descriptions of activities to be used in these workforms. Standardizing the vocabulary that describes a library's activities eases data collection.

Factors to Consider When Completing Workforms 5–6

1. The degree of precision you will require about a staff member's day varies greatly. An informed estimate based on experience or established standards provides enough information to do an activity-level numeric analysis. Workforms 5 and 6 help you develop general "guesstimates" with which to work. *To capture more-precise data at the task level, use Workforms 7 and 8.*

2. Staff may be uncomfortable being asked to create estimates. Some people have a very good sense of how they spend their time and an equally good sense of proportion. It isn't hard for them to think in terms of percentages of time or hours a week they might do something. For others, this is a very difficult exercise. They have a hard time thinking in terms of percentages of time spent on activities and are unclear about how to handle those activities that come up only occasionally or that consume a great deal of time during only one portion of the year.

3. It is important that everyone understand these are *informed guesses* that will be used in developing activity-level numeric measures. Minor variations between these estimates and more-precise data that may be collected in another way at another time are not significant for this analysis.

Instructions

Purpose of Workform 5

Use this workform to estimate the percentage of time your staff members spend on each of their assigned activities.

Who Should Complete Workform 5?

Workform 5 should be completed by the supervisor in a work unit. Alternately, a separate workform, Workform 6, may be completed by each staff member in a work unit to develop this information.

Sources of Data for Workform 5

1. Standards or policies (formal or informal) related to work may provide the information needed for Workform 5. For example, if your library has a policy of staff spending half of their time on public desks and half of their time in backroom work, meetings, etc., that standard may provide sufficient information to complete this workform.

2. A discussion among the staff members themselves may develop a consensus that can be reported on Workform 5.

3. Asking individual staff to complete Workform 6 and then reporting the average of the results in Workform 5 is another way to develop these estimates.

Factors to Consider When Completing Workform 5

1. Remember that this is an *estimate*, not a detailed analysis of a unit's or an individual's work. List large activities such as "staff the desk" and "shelve materials" or "process new materials" and "work on database." If more-precise data at the task level is needed, use either Workform 7, Self-Report Log, or Workform 8, Direct Observation Log, to capture the necessary information.

2. Some activities occur occasionally rather than regularly. Look for ways to combine these activities into a larger activity. For example, one week a month a staff member may spend off-desk hours weeding while the other three weeks are

spent ordering new books, reviewing patron purchase requests and hold lists for additional copies needed, and reviewing newly received materials before they are shelved. All of these could be grouped and reported as "collection maintenance." Developing bookmarks and brochures, working with community groups, and managing displays could all be grouped together as "marketing." This is only an informed guess; don't spend a lot of time on it.

To Complete Workform 5

1. **Item A**   Write the location and/or work unit whose work is reported on this workform.

2. **Column B**   On the lines provided, list the primary activities performed by the unit. Activities will be sets of tasks that generally take 10 percent or more of the work time of any staff member in the work unit.

   Standard terms describing activities may have been developed by the library as a part of this data-gathering process. If so, use those terms here. Check with the person who asked you to complete this workform to determine if standard terms exist.

3. **Column C**   Write each job classification in the unit—one in each column C. If you have more than three classifications, copy and link to this sheet additional columns for C and D.

4. **Column D**   For each line in line with an activity listed, in the column D for each job classification enter the percentage of time that full- and part-time staff spend on that activity. (*Note:* There are two D columns for each column C.)

5. **Item E**   Total each of the D columns. The total should equal 100%.

Factor to Consider When Reviewing Workform 5

Some activities occur seasonally rather than year-round. If the work unit being reported on has a high degree of seasonal variance (i.e., a children's department in which the bulk of programming is done in the summer), you may want to complete estimates for the different seasons to get a better picture of the work.

WORKFORM 5 Analysis of Staff Time: Work Unit
Estimate of Time Spent on Activities

A. Location and/or work unit: _____

B. Activities	**C. Job Classification:** ___		**C. Job Classification:** ___		**C. Job Classification:** ___	
	D. % of Full-Time Staff	**D. % of Part-Time Staff**	**D. % of Full-Time Staff**	**D. % of Part-Time Staff**	**D. % of Full-Time Staff**	**D. % of Part-Time Staff**
1.						
2.						
3.						
4.						
5.						
6.						
7.						
8.						
9.						
10.						
11.						
12.						
13.						
E. Totals						

Completed by _____ Date completed _____

Source of data _____ Library _____

WORKFORM 6   Analysis of Staff Time: Individual Estimate of Time Spent on Activities

Instructions

Purpose of Workform 6

Use this workform to estimate the percentage of time you spend on each of your assigned activities.

Who Should Complete Workform 6?

Each staff member in a work unit should complete Workform 6.

Source of Data for Workform 6

Your assigned activities are the source of information for this workform.

Factors to Consider When Completing Workform 6

1. Although you do many things in a typical day, week, or month, the purpose of this workform is to identify blocks of time in your schedule, not each discrete action you take. An activity is a set of tasks that generally take 10% or more of your work time. List large activities such as "staff the desk" and "shelve materials" or "process new materials" and "work on database."

2. Remember that this is an *estimate* of how you spend a typical work period, not a detailed analysis of your work. Look for ways to combine smaller activities into a larger activity. For example, "make schedules, deposit cash, turn on machines" might all be combined into an activity called "supervisory tasks."

3. Some activities occur occasionally rather than regularly. Look for ways to combine these activities into a larger activity. For example, one week a month off-desk hours may be spent weeding while the other three weeks are spent ordering new books, reviewing patron purchase requests and hold lists for additional copies needed, and reviewing newly received materials before they are shelved. All of these activities could be grouped and reported as "collection

maintenance." Developing bookmarks and brochures, working with community groups, and managing displays could all be grouped together as "marketing." This is only an informed guess; don't spend a lot of time on it.

4. Standard terms describing activities may have been developed by the library as a part of this data-gathering process. If so, use those terms here. Check with the person who asked you to complete this workform to determine if standard terms exist.

To Complete Workform 6

1. **Item A**   Write the location and/or work unit where you work.

2. **Item B**   Write your job classification and check the box for FT if you are a full-time employee or PT if you are a part-time employee.

3. **Item C**   Check the box for the period of time your estimates cover.

4. **Column D**   On the lines provided list the primary activities you perform in your job. Remember, activities will be sets of tasks that generally take 10% or more of the work time. Use any standard terms that may have been developed by the library to describe staff activities.

5. **Column E**   For each line with an activity listed in column D, enter the percentage of time that you spend on the activity.

6. **Item F**   Total column E. The total should equal 100%.

Factors to Consider When Reviewing Workform 6

Some activities occur seasonally rather than year-round. If the staff members providing these estimates work in a unit with a high degree of seasonal variance (i.e., a children's department in which the bulk of programming is done in the summer), you may want to ask them to complete estimates for the different seasons to get a better picture of the work.

WORKFORM 6 Analysis of Staff Time: Individual Estimate of Time Spent on Activities

A. Location and/or work unit: _____

B. Job classification: _____   ☐ FT   ☐ PT

C. Period of time: ☐ daily   ☐ weekly   ☐ monthly

D. Activities	E. % of Time Spent
1.	
2.	
3.	
4.	
5.	
6.	
7.	
8.	
9.	
10.	
11.	
12.	
13.	
14.	
15.	
F. Total	100%

Completed by _____ Date completed _____

Source of data _____ Library _____

General Instructions

Purpose of Workforms 7–8

Use these workforms to identify the tasks a staff member performs during a workday.

Who Should Complete Workforms 7–8?

These workforms should be completed either by an observer (Workform 8) or by the staff members whose work is being studied (Workform 7). Staff may have a difficult time completing self-reporting workforms accurately while working at a public desk, so observation will work best for tasks related to direct public service. Either observation or self-reporting will work for off-desk activities.

Sources of Data for Workforms 7–8

1. Either self-reports from staff or the observations of staff provide the basis for this information.

2. Standardizing the vocabulary that describes a library's tasks eases data collection. Workform 4 can be used to develop common terms or descriptions of tasks to be used in these workforms.

Factors to Consider When Completing Workforms 7–8

1. The degree of precision you will require in the numbers varies greatly. Occasionally an informed estimate based on experience or established standards provides enough information to do an activity-level numeric analysis. Workforms 7 and 8 collect detailed information on the tasks in a staff member's day, while Workforms 5 and 6 help you develop a very general "guesstimate" of the activities a staff member is assigned to perform. Use the workforms that give you the level of precision you need.

2. Staff being observed may be nervous. Their apprehensions need to be allayed by informing them that the library is looking at work *tasks*, not staff performance.

3. Note that each workform has separate instructions.

WORKFORM 7 **Recording Staff Tasks: Self-Report Log**

Instructions

Purpose of Workform 7

Use this workform to identify the tasks a staff member performs during the day.

Who Should Complete Workform 7?

Every person who performs tasks associated with the activity under study should complete this workform. For example, if you are studying circulation, it is not necessary for reference staff to complete this workform unless they regularly work at the circulation desk as a part of their normal activities.

Factor to Consider When Completing Workform 7

Keep a running log of your time and tasks. Trying to remember what you did some hours earlier will result in an inaccurate record. For this reason it may be easier and more accurate to record time spent on public desks through observation (Workform 8) rather than through self-reporting.

To Complete Workform 7

An example of a completed workform is provided as a guide to assist you in completing this workform.

1. **Items A–D**   Complete the information on the workform.

   Item A   Write the location and/or work unit where you work.

   Item B   Write the day and the date you complete this log.

   Item C   Write your name.

   Item D   Write your job classification.

2. **Column E**   Fill in the hours of your shift. You will be recording your time in 15-minute intervals during the workday.

   Note that there are 8 hours of time available on the workform. Do *not* record the time you spend on your lunch or dinner break, but *do* record your other work breaks.

3. **Column F**   Write what you did during the time period being recorded. If the task covered more than one 15-minute block, draw an arrow down column F to the time block when the activity concluded. For example, if you processed books from 10:15 to 11:00, write "processed books" in the block next to 10:15 and draw an arrow to the line above the row for 11:00. (See the example of the completed workform.)

   If you performed *more than one activity* during the 15-minute interval, record *only* the task that occupied the most time except as instructed below.

   Standard terms describing tasks may have been developed by the library as a part of this data-gathering process. If so, use those terms here. Check with the person who asked you to complete this workform to determine if standard terms exist.

   When assigned to a public service desk, it is possible to perform more activities other than direct assistance during slow periods. If you spend a block of desk time primarily doing something else, record that as well.

Factor to Consider When Reviewing Workform 7

Time of year can affect tasks. For example, children's programming may be more frequent in the summer, or ordering new books may be greatly reduced in the last month of the fiscal year. If seasonal variances exist, you may want to have staff complete this workform several times during the year to develop a more complete picture of their work tasks.

WORKFORM 7   **Recording Staff Tasks: Self-Report Log—*Example***

A. Location and/or work unit: Ash Branch Reference

B. Date and day of report: Monday 10/4

C. Name: Becky Boyd

D. Job classification: Librarian I

E. Time	**F. Task**	**E. Time**	**F. Task**
9:00	On desk	2:00	Meeting
9:15	On desk/read reviews	2:15	→
9:30	→	2:30	
9:45	On desk	2:45	
10:00	Develop bibliography	3:00	Weed/reorder damaged materials
10:15	→	3:15	→
10:30	Break	3:30	
10:45	Develop bibliography	3:45	Break
11:00	→	4:00	On desk
11:15	Create orders	4:15	
11:30	→	4:30	
11:45	→	4:45	
12:00	On desk	5:00	
12:15	→	5:15	
12:30		5:30	
12:45		5:45	→

Completed by Becky Boyd

Date completed 10/4

Source of data self

Library Ash Branch

Recording Staff Tasks: Self-Report Log

A. Location and/or work unit: _____

B. Date and day of report: _____

C. Name: _____

D. Job classification: _____

E. Time	F. Task	E. Time	F. Task
:00		:00	
:15		:15	
:30		:30	
:45		:45	
:00		:00	
:15		:15	
:30		:30	
:45		:45	
:00		:00	
:15		:15	
:30		:30	
:45		:45	
:00		:00	
:15		:15	
:30		:30	
:45		:45	

Completed by _____ Date completed _____

Source of data _____ Library _____

Purpose of Workform 8

Use this workform to identify the tasks staff members of a particular work unit perform during the day. This workform will give you an overview of the tasks performed in a work unit, not an overview of the tasks performed by each member of that unit. To develop information on an individual staff member's day, use Workform 7.

Source of Data for Workform 8

Direct observations of staff as they perform their jobs provide the information for this workform. Multiple observations will be needed to form a reasonable picture of the tasks in a work unit.

Factors to Consider When Completing Workform 8

1. *When should observations be done?* Ideally, observations should be done during all of the times the work unit is operating. For public service units, this includes nights and weekends.

   Make some observations at times during the hour rather than on the hour or half hour when they are more likely to be expected. Subsequent observations should occur at different minutes in the hours following. The point is to randomize the times at which observations are made.

2. *How many observations should be done?* The number of individual observations depend on the size of the staff. To ensure reliability, a minimum of 30 observations should be made in a unit each day. The greater the number of staff in a unit, the larger the number of observations you will need. Follow this guide:

Number of Staff	Number of Single Observations
2–10	30
11–20	33–40
21–30	42–60
31+	62

   The number of observations per person depends on staff size to a large extent. For example, a staff of 3 would each be observed 10 times during a day. A staff of 10 would each be observed 3 times during a day. All employees working the

same number of hours should be observed the same number of times to ensure an unbiased set of observations. Observations of part-time employees should be prorated according to the number of hours in their shift.

3. *How long should the observation period be?* The observation period should cover at least three days. The period can be done in a single week or over three weeks. The observation period should allow for all employees working those days to be observed.

   If more than one observation period is planned, the days of the week and hours of observation should be different from previous observation periods.

4. Staff being observed may be nervous. Their apprehensions need to be allayed by informing them that the library is looking at tasks and activities, not at their performance.

5. Each person assigned to the unit under observation should be recorded.

6. Standardizing the vocabulary that describes tasks and steps eases data collection. You may want to start by having staff complete Workform 4 to identify common terms or descriptions of tasks and steps that can be used in this workform. Provide those terms and their definitions to observers by giving them a copy of completed Workform 4 when you ask them to complete this workform. Ask the people who complete this workform to use only those standardized terms.

7. Observation periods should be repeated several times during the study period to accumulate the data needed to see the larger picture of activities.

To Complete Workform 8

1. **Items A–C**   Complete the information on the workform.

   Item A   Write the day of the week on which the observations are made.

   Item B   Write the date of the observations.

   Item C   Write the location and/or work unit being observed.

2. **Item D**   Record the name and job classification of each staff member working on the day of the observations.

3. **Column E**   Either record the exact time (10:10) or the hour. Using the hour is easier for observers. Whichever you choose, be consistent.

(Continued)

Instructions

4. **Column F**   Each staff member on duty is to be observed. Write the name and job classification of the staff member being observed on the Observation Log and refer to it when recording in column F.

5. **Column G**   Indicate the location of the staff member being observed. For staff who cannot be located, write "not located" in this column. Use the letters *OBLB* for staff who are out of the building on library business.

6. **Column H**   If you are not sure what the person is doing, either ask the person or leave the line blank. If the staff member is assigned to a public service desk and there is no activity, write "no activity."

Factor to Consider When Reviewing Workform 8

The time of year can affect activities, as can the time of day. For example, children's programming may be more frequent in the summer.

WORKFORM 8 Recording Staff Tasks: Direct Observation Log

A. Day of the week: _____

B. Date of observation: _____

C. Location and/or work unit observed: _____

D. Staff on duty on this date:

1. Name: _____ Classification: _____
2. Name: _____ Classification: _____
3. Name: _____ Classification: _____
4. Name: _____ Classification: _____
5. Name: _____ Classification: _____
6. Name: _____ Classification: _____
7. Name: _____ Classification: _____
8. Name: _____ Classification: _____
9. Name: _____ Classification: _____
10. Name: _____ Classification: _____
11. Name: _____ Classification: _____
12. Name: _____ Classification: _____
13. Name: _____ Classification: _____
14. Name: _____ Classification: _____
15. Name: _____ Classification: _____
16. Name: _____ Classification: _____
17. Name: _____ Classification: _____
18. Name: _____ Classification: _____
19. Name: _____ Classification: _____
20. Name: _____ Classification: _____

(Continued)

WORKFORM 8 **Recording Staff Tasks: Direct Observation Log (Cont.)**

E. Time	F. Name/Job Classification	G. Location	H. Task

Completed by _____ Date completed _____

Source of data _____ Library _____

General Instructions

Purposes of Workform 9

1. Use this workform to identify all of the steps involved in performing a task.

   You may find that you use this workform multiple times during a workload analysis project. In studying work from the task to the step level, you may choose to elevate one step you previously identified to the level of a task and break it into its own set of steps. Alternately, you may find you want to reduce the number of steps you measure in a task by aggregating multiple steps into one step for data-collection purposes. See the examples of the completed workforms for clarification on this point.

2. The information captured on this workform can also be used to standardize the steps in a task or to develop a common set of terms that describe a task. Standardizing the vocabulary that describes a library's tasks eases data collection. These common terms or descriptions of steps and tasks can be used in other workforms.

Who Should Complete Workform 9?

The workform should be completed either by an observer or by the person performing the task. The work of everybody who performs the task in the unit under consideration should be noted by the observer or reported by the staff involved to show the sequence of steps in performing each person's part.

Sources of Data for Workform 9

1. The tasks to be studied with this workform may be identified from Workforms 3 or 4 or from discussions with staff who do the work you are studying.

2. Either self-reports from people performing steps for this task or observations of persons performing the task provide the basis for this information.

   Observations can be more accurate than self-descriptions because some steps might not be recorded. Furthermore, although a procedure manual may list the steps involved in performing the task, the instructions may not be followed by individual staff.

3. Note that observers and self-reports have separate instructions that follow these general instructions.

Factors to Consider When Reviewing Workform 9

1. Why is this task done at all? Does it contribute to achieving the library's goals?

2. Are these the right steps to accomplish the task?

3. Do you understand the reason for doing each step? Are the reasons still valid or are they based on previous circumstances that may have changed?

4. Are the steps being done in the right order?

5. Do the steps listed in the workform give you the level of detail you need? Would the staff member or observer be capable of capturing measurement data for each step listed? The tendency of staff completing this workform is to be too detailed in their analysis of the steps involved in a task. It may be useful to consider aggregating some of the reported steps, particularly the self-reported steps, into groups that you can time as if they were one step.

6. Some tasks may consist of a single step. If the steps in a task are done in a particular sequence for each occurrence of the task, you may not be able to measure each step separately. For example, entering item data into an automation system includes entering multiple pieces of data. Timing the entry of each piece is difficult and doesn't give you useful information. It is more useful to know that over a period of 15 minutes, one staff member entered 25 items into the database.

WORKFORM 9   Analysis of a Task (Observation)

Instructions

Purpose of Workform 9

Use this workform to identify all of the steps involved in performing a task. If, instead, you are seeking to create a complete record of a staff member's tasks through observation during a particular *period of time*, Workform 8, Recording Staff Tasks: Direct Observation Log, and Workform 12, Time Spent on Public Desks, are designed for that purpose. Workform 7, Recording Staff Tasks: Self-Report Log, can be used by staff to make a chronological record of their tasks throughout a day.

Source of Data for Workform 9

Direct observations as recorded by designated observers provide the information for this workform.

Factors to Consider When Completing Workform 9

1. Choose the observers for each unit to be observed. The observers may be supervisors, staff members, or people from outside the unit. However, it is necessary that observers be able to recognize individual staff members. Observers may also need access to nonpublic areas in the library.

2. Staff should be informed that the observations will occur but not when they will occur to avoid skewing the observations.

3. Staff being observed may be nervous. Their apprehensions need to be allayed by informing them that the library is looking at steps in tasks, not at their individual performance.

4. If the same tasks are performed by many persons in the work unit, it is important to know how the steps are performed by each person.

5. Use a separate workform for each person who performs the task or a portion of the task. For example, if the staff member both checks out and checks in materials, use a separate workform to record first one, then the other task. This workform is *not* for recording a chronological analysis of how a staff member spends his or her time but for recording the steps in a single task. You will need to observe multiple occurrences of a single task to be sure you have identified all of the steps.

6. If you don't know or can't figure out what a particular step is, don't ask the staff you are observing. Make a note about your confusion so that the question can be raised later.

7. Data about work passed along from person to person should be compiled to produce a summary of the steps involved in the task. Use a separate workform for each person involved.

To Complete Workform 9

An example of a completed workform is provided as a guide to assist you in completing this workform.

1. **Item A**   Check the box for observer report.

2. **Item B**   Write the location and work unit in which the task is done.

3. **Item C**   Write the name and job classification of the staff member you are observing.

4. **Item D**   Enter the task being analyzed and describe in general terms the staff member's part in performing the task.

   If more than one person does this task, standard terms to describe tasks may have been developed by the library as a part of this data-gathering process. If so, use those terms here. Check with the person who asked you to complete this workform to determine if standard terms exist.

5. **Item E**   Identify what gets counted in this staff member's part of this task. For example, the staff member may be counting trucks of materials shelved, items checked out, orders placed, etc. In other words, how does the staff member calculate the accomplishment of this task?

   If, at present, there is no reported output from this task, enter what you think could or should be reported to count the output of this task. Start by writing "Suggested count:" so that people using this workform will know that this data is a suggestion, not a number the library currently collects.

6. **Item F**   Identify the first thing that the staff member does to start this task.

7. **Item G**   List—in sequence—all of the steps performed by this staff member for this task. Use another sheet of paper if necessary, but number all of the steps in sequence. There should be no discontinuities in the steps, and the ending point of one step should be the starting point of the next step.

8. **Item H**   Identify the end point of the task. The end point could be passing the task to another person. If so, name the person.

9. **Item I**   Check the box for Yes if you think this process should be changed in some way. If you check Yes, attach a separate sheet with your suggestions. Be as specific as you can be about the changes you recommend. If no change is needed, check the box for No.

Factors to Consider When Reviewing Workform 9

See this section in the general instructions for Workform 9.

WORKFORM 9 Analysis of a Task (Observation)—*Example*

A. ☐ Self-report ☒ Observer report

B. Location and/or work unit: Main Library reference desk

C. Name and job classification of person performing the task: Mary Morris, Librarian I

D. Task: Selecting materials—choosing materials and verifying and preparing orders

E. What gets counted: Number of titles ordered

F. Starting point of task: Gather review materials

G. List the steps involved in sequence

1. Read review

2. Check online catalog for duplication

3. Complete order card, including number to order and suggested distribution

4. _____

5. _____

6. _____

7. _____

8. _____

9. _____

10. _____

H. End point of task: Send order cards to department head for review and approval

I. Is there anything you would change in this process? ☐ Yes ☒ No

If yes, attach a separate sheet to this workform outlining your suggestions for changes.

Completed by Zeke Anders   Date completed 10/20

Source of data observation   Library Main Library, Tree Co. PL.

WORKFORM 9 Analysis of a Task (Self-Report)

Instructions

Purpose of Workform 9

Use this workform to identify the steps involved in performing a task.

Sources of Data for Workform 9

Every person who performs steps associated with the task under consideration provides the data for this workform. Each person is to list in sequence the steps he or she does when performing the task.

Factors to Consider When Completing Workform 9

1. Write down the steps as you go along. This way you are unlikely to forget any part of the process.

2. Use a separate workform for each task. For example, if you both check out and check in materials, use a separate workform to record first one, then the other task. This workform is *not* for recording a chronological analysis of how you spend your time but for recording the steps in a single task. You may need to observe yourself during multiple occurrences of a single task to be sure you have identified all of the steps.

3. If the task you are recording branches into different actions based on a decision point (i.e., you scan a patron's card to check out materials and do one thing if there are no blocks or something different if there are blocks), you may need to complete two separate copies of Workform 9. Ask the person who gave you the workform about what level of detail is required.

4. It is important that each person record his or her own steps in completing a task. Please do not copy lists of steps from others in your department who are completing this workform. Record your own steps.

To Complete Workform 9

An example of a completed workform is provided as a guide to assist you in completing this workform.

1. **Item A** Check the self-report box.
2. **Item B** Write the location and/or work unit in which the task is done.
3. **Item C** Write your name and job classification.
4. **Item D** Enter the task being analyzed and describe in general terms your part in performing the task.

   If people other than you do this task, standard terms to describe tasks may have been developed by the library as a part of this data-gathering process. If so, use those terms here. Check with the person who asked you to complete this workform to determine if standard terms exist.

5. **Item E** Identify what gets counted and reported in your part of this task. For example, you may be counting trucks of materials shelved, items checked out, orders placed, etc. In other words, how do you report the accomplishment of your part of this task?

   If, at present, there is no reported output from this task, enter what you think could or should be reported to count the output of this task. Start by writing "Suggested count:" so that people using this workform will know that the information is a suggestion, not a number the library currently collects.

6. **Item F** Identify the first step that you take to start this task.

7. **Item G** List—in sequence—all of the steps you perform for this task. Use another sheet of paper if necessary, but number all of the steps in sequence. There should be no discontinuities in the steps, and the ending point of one step should be the starting point to the next step. **List only the steps related to this particular task.** Even though you do other tasks, this workform is collecting information on only *one* task.

   If you have been asked to collect data on more than one task, use a separate workform for each task.

8. **Item H** Identify the end point of the task. The end point could be passing the task to another person. If so, name the person.

9. **Item I** Check the box for Yes if you think this process should be changed in some way. If you check Yes, attach a separate sheet with your suggestions. Be as specific as you can be about the changes you recommend. If no change is needed, check the box for No.

Factors to Consider When Reviewing Workform 9

See this section in the general instructions for Workform 9.

WORKFORM 9   Analysis of a Task (Self-Report)—*Example*

A. ☒ Self-report   ☐ Observer report

B. Location and/or work unit: <u>Main Library reference desk</u>

C. Name and job classification of person performing the task: <u>Mary Morris, Librarian I</u>

D. Task: <u>Reference and information services at public desk—direct public service</u>

E. What gets counted: <u>Number of reference questions, number of directional queries</u>

F. Starting point of task: <u>Approach of patron to desk/telephone call</u>

G. List the steps involved in sequence

1. <u>Greet patron/answer phone/determine type of question</u>

2. <u>Provide answer or referral to source of information</u>

3. <u>Confirm that patron is satisfied with answer</u>

4. <u>Record the type of question on statistics sheet</u>

5.

6.

7.

8.

9.

10.

H. End point of task: <u>Departure of patron/end of phone call</u>

I. Is there anything you would change in this process?   ☐ Yes   ☒ No

If yes, attach a separate sheet to this workform outlining your suggestions for changes.

Completed by <u>Mary Morris</u>   Date completed <u>10/10</u>

Source of data <u>self</u>   Library <u>Main Library, Tree Co. PL.</u>

WORKFORM 9 **Analysis of a Task**

A. ☐ Self-report ☐ Observer report

B. Location and/or work unit: _____

C. Name and job classification of person performing the task: _____

D. Task: _____

E. What gets counted: _____

F. Starting point of task: _____

G. List the steps involved in sequence

1. _____

2. _____

3. _____

4. _____

5. _____

6. _____

7. _____

8. _____

9. _____

10. _____

H. End point of task: _____

I. Is there anything you would change in this process? ☐ Yes ☐ No

If yes, attach a separate sheet to this workform outlining your suggestions for changes.

Completed by _____ Date completed _____

Source of data _____ Library _____

Instructions

Purpose of Workform 10

Use this workform to identify the relationship of outputs to the time spent during the performance of the steps in an input-driven task.

Who Should Complete Workform 10?

The workform may be completed by the person performing the steps in the task or by an observer. The work of each person in the unit under consideration who performs these steps should be reported.

Sources of Data for Workform 10

Self-reports from people performing the steps or observers watching as the task is performed provide the basis for this information.

Factors to Consider When Completing Workform 10

1. An input-driven task is one where you have control over the number of outputs required and the level of effort expended to produce those outputs.

2. This workform is designed to assist in determining how much time each of the steps in a task takes. This is *not* a workform for determining how a staff member spends his or her day, Workforms 7 or 8 collect that information.

3. Standardizing the vocabulary that describes the steps eases data collection if more than one person performs a task. To ease comparison of information from multiple staff, you may want to start by having staff complete Workform 9 to identify common terms or descriptions of steps that can be used in this workform. Provide those terms and their definitions to staff by giving them a copy of completed Workform 4 when you ask them to complete this workform.

To Complete Workform 10

An example of a completed workform is provided as a guide to assist you in completing this workform.

1. **Item A**   Identify the facility and/or work unit in which the task is done.
2. **Item B**   Write your name.
3. **Item C**   Identify the task you are recording.

Standard terms describing tasks and steps may have been developed by the library as a part of this data-gathering process. If so, use those terms here. Check

with the person who asked you to complete this workform to determine if standard terms exist.

4. **Column D**   Write in the first step you do (or observe) in performing this task. Use the standard terms for each step if the library has developed standard terms.

Complete each row in the chart before you begin the next step in this task. When you begin a new step, write it in the next row in column D. (See the example of a completed Workform 10.)

5. **Column E**   Write the time you begin each step.
6. **Column F**   Write the time you end each step.
7. **Column G**   Calculate the elapsed time between the beginning and the end of the step. You may make this calculation as you record your steps or at the end of your data collection before you submit the workform. Express the elapsed time in minutes.

8. **Column H**   Count the number of outputs you completed in this step during the time recorded. Note that if your step involves dispersing outputs to other locations (shelving books, delivering mail, packing crates, etc.), you will need to count the number you will be handling *before* you disperse the items.

9. **Column I**   Divide the number of minutes of elapsed time by the number of outputs completed (G/H). If the answer is greater than 1, express the results as "X minutes per Y," where X is your result and Y is the output.

If the answer is less than 1, recalculate your results by dividing the number of outputs completed by the number of minutes of elapsed time (H/G). Express the result as "Y outputs per minute."

These calculations may be done at the end of your data collection before you submit the workform.

Factors to Consider When Reviewing Workform 10

1. Do you understand the reason for each step listed in the task?
2. Can you identify what each step contributes to the customer's satisfaction with the output?
3. Does the amount of time each step takes seem reasonable to you?
4. If you have copies of this workform for this task from multiple people, do the steps take approximately the same amount of time, regardless of who is doing the work?

WORKFORM 10 Time Spent on an Input-Driven Task—*Example*

A. Location and/or work unit: __Ash Branch__

B. Name of person performing the task: __Tressa Jones__

C. Task: __Processing hold materials for pickup__

D. Step	E. Start Time	F. End Time	G. Elapsed Time	H. Number Completed	I. Output Rate (G/H or H/G)
1. Receive and organize hold materials	12:45	1:15	30 min.	35	1.16 per minute or 70 per hour
2. Phone or e-mail patrons	1:15	1:50	35 min.	35	1 per minute or 60 per hour
3. Label materials with patron names	1:50	2:10	20 min.	35	1.75 per minute or 105 per hour
4. Arrange materials being held on book truck by patron last name	2:10	2:20	10 min.	35	3.5 per minute or 210 per hour
5.					
6.					
7.					
8.					
9.					
10.					

Completed by ___T. Jones___   Date completed ___10/10___

Source of data ___self-report___   Library ___Ash Branch___

WORKFORM 10 **Time Spent on an Input-Driven Task**

A. Location and/or work unit: _____

B. Name of person performing the task: _____

C. Task: _____

D. Step	E. Start Time	F. End Time	G. Elapsed Time	H. Number Completed	I. Output Rate (G/H or H/G)
1.					
2.					
3.					
4.					
5.					
6.					
7.					
8.					
9.					
10.					

Completed by _____ Date completed _____

Source of data _____ Library _____

Instructions

WORKFORM 11   Time Spent on a Demand-Driven Task

Purpose of Workform 11

Use this workform to identify the average amount of time spent on each step in a demand-driven task.

Who Should Complete Workform 11?

The workform may be completed by the person performing the task or by an observer. The work of each person in the unit under consideration who performs the task should be reported.

Source of Data for Workform 11

Self-reports from people performing the task or observers watching as the task is performed provide the basis for this information.

Factors to Consider When Completing Workform 11

1. Note that you will most likely be using aggregated steps on this workform. Workform 4 includes more information on aggregated steps.

2. This workform is designed to assist in determining how much time each of the step types takes during a given period of measurement. This is *not* a workform for determining how a staff member spends a portion of his or her day. Workform 7 or 8 can be used to gather that information.

3. Standardizing the vocabulary that describes the steps eases data collection if more than one person performs a task. To ease comparison of information from multiple staff, you may want to start by having staff complete Workform 9 to identify common terms or descriptions of tasks and steps that can be used in this workform. Provide those terms and their definitions to staff or observers by giving them a copy of completed Workform 4 when you ask them to complete this workform. Ask the people who complete this workform to use only standardized terms.

To Complete Workform 11

An example of a completed workform is provided as a guide to assist you in completing this workform.

1. **Item A**   Write the facility and/or work unit in which the task is done.

2. **Item B**   Write the task being recorded or observed.

3. **Item C**   Write the name of the person whose work is recorded on this workform.

4. **Item D**   Write the day of the week and time of day during which these steps are being recorded.

5. **Column E**   Write the first step you do (or observe). Standard terms describing steps may have been developed by the library as a part of this data-gathering process. If so, use those terms here. Check with the person who asked you to complete this workform if you haven't been given a list of standard terms. If the step being done or observed does not match any of the standard terms, write "Other."

6. **Column F**   Write the time as each step begins.

7. **Column G**   Write the time as each step ends.

8. **Column H**   Calculate the elapsed time between the beginning and the end of the step. You may make this calculation as you record the tasks or at the end of your data collection before you submit the workform. Express the elapsed time in minutes.

9. **Column I**   Review the steps in column E. Write each *unique* step on one of the numbered lines in column I. For example, if you have recorded "direct patron assistance" 15 times and "PC assistance" 5 times in column E, you would enter "direct patron assistance" and "PC assistance" once each in column I.

10. **Column J**   Count the number of times the step in column I was completed during the recorded period, and enter that number in column J in the same row in which the step is listed.

11. **Column K**   Add the elapsed times from column H for all of the occurrences of the listed step and enter the total number of elapsed minutes for this step in column K.

12. **Column L**   Divide column K by column J for each row, and enter the result in that row in column L.

Factors to Consider When Reviewing Workform 11

1. Do you understand the reason for each step listed in the task?

2. Can you identify what each step contributes to the customer's satisfaction with the outputs?

3. Does the amount of time spent on each type of step seem reasonable to you? Does it represent the service mix you expected to find in this task? For example, if you are reviewing the steps in the task of providing service at the reference desk, do you think the balance between desk work and direct public interactions is appropriate?

4. How often does "Other" appear in Column E? If it appears frequently, you may not have developed a complete or accurate list of the steps being taken in this task. You may want to create a new set of step descriptions and collect the data

WORKFORM 11 Time Spent on a Demand-Driven Task

A. Location and/or work unit: _____

B. Task: _____

C. Name of person recording/observed: _____

D. Day and time of record/observation: _____

E. Step	F. Start Time	G. End Time	H. Elapsed Time
1.			
2.			
3.			
4.			
5.			
6.			
7.			
8.			
9.			
10.			
11.			
12.			
13.			
14.			
15.			
16.			

(Continued)

WORKFORM 11 Time Spent on a Demand-Driven Task (Cont.)

Summary of Steps

I. Step Type	J. Number of Occurrences	K. Total Elapsed Time	L. Time per Occurrence (K/J)
1.			
2.			
3.			
4.			
5.			
6.			
7.			
8.			
9.			
10.			
11.			
12.			
13.			
14.			
15.			
16.			

Completed by _____ Date completed _____

Source of data _____ Library _____

Instructions

Purpose of Workform 12

Use this workform to identify the amount of time spent on tasks at public desks.

Who Should Complete Workform 12?

The workform should be completed by an observer. The work of each person on the public desk during the period of time recorded should be reported.

Source of Data for Workform 12

Observations as the task is performed provide the data for this information.

Factors to Consider When Completing Workform 12

1. Note that you will most likely be recording information on aggregated tasks on this workform. Workform 4 includes more information on aggregated tasks.

2. This workform is designed to assist in determining how much time each of the task types takes during a given period of measurement. This is *not* a workform for determining how a staff member spends a portion of his or her day. Workform 7 or 8 can be used to gather that information.

3. Standardizing the vocabulary that describes the tasks eases data collection of public desk tasks. You may want to start by having staff complete Workform 9 to identify common terms or descriptions of tasks that can be used in this workform. Provide those terms and their definitions to observers by giving them a copy of completed Workform 4 when you ask them to complete this workform. Ask the people who complete this workform to use only standardized terms.

4. You should develop a shorthand representation for each of the tasks, i.e., *P* for patron assistance and *W* for wait time tasks, since you will miss tasks if you try to write detailed explanations for each one.

5. A stopwatch will be very useful to help you record tasks at a busy desk. Rather than recording start and stop times you can record elapsed times for tasks. A digital readout will be the easiest to read and record.

6. For a very busy desk with more than one staff member, you may want to have an observer for each staff member so you can accurately capture the tasks each staff member does.

To Complete Workform 12

1. **Item A**   Write the facility and/or work unit in which the observed tasks are done.

2. **Item B**   Write the specific desk where tasks are being observed.

3. **Item C**   Write the name of the person or persons whose work is recorded on this workform.

4. **Item D**   Write the day of the week and time period during which these tasks are being recorded.

5. **Column E**   Write the time as each task begins or start the stopwatch.

6. **Column F**   Write the time as each task ends or stop the stopwatch.

7. **Column G**   Record the elapsed time from the stopwatch or calculate the elapsed time between the beginning and the end of the task. If you are calculating the elapsed time, you should make this calculation at the end of your data collection before you submit the workform. Express the elapsed time in minutes.

8. **Column H**   Write in the shorthand description of the task you observed. Standard terms describing tasks may have been developed by the library as a part of this data-gathering process. Use those terms here. Check with the person who asked you to complete this workform if you haven't been given a list of standard terms. If the task being observed does not match any of the standard terms, write *O* for "other."

9. **Column I**   Review the tasks in column H. Write each unique task on one of the numbered lines in column I.

10. **Column J**   Count the number of times the task in column I was completed during the recorded period, and enter that number in column J in the same row in which the task is listed.

11. **Column K**   Add the elapsed times from column G for all of the occurrences of each listed task, and enter the total number of elapsed minutes for each task in column K.

12. **Column L**   Divide column K by column J for each row, and enter the result in that row in column L.

Factors to Consider When Reviewing Workform 12

1. Does the amount of time spent on each task seem reasonable to you? Does it represent the service mix you expected to find at this desk? For example, do you think the balance between wait time desk work and direct public interactions is appropriate?

2. How often does "other" appear in column H? If it appears frequently, you may not have developed a complete or accurate list of the tasks being done at this desk. You may want to create a new set of task descriptions and collect the data again to more completely describe the tasks at this desk.

151

WORKFORM 12 Time Spent on Public Desks

A. Location and/or work unit: _____

B. Desk: _____

C. Name(s) of person(s) observed: _____

D. Day and time period of observation: _____

	E. Start Time	F. End Time	G. Elapsed Time	H. Task
1.				
2.				
3.				
4.				
5.				
6.				
7.				
8.				
9.				
10.				
11.				
12.				
13.				
14.				
15.				
16.				

(Continued)

Summary of Tasks:

I. Tasks	J. Number of Occurrences	K. Total Elapsed Time	L. Time per Occurrence (K/J)
1.			
2.			
3.			
4.			
5.			
6.			
7.			
8.			
9.			
10.			
11.			
12.			
13.			
14.			
15.			
16.			

Completed by _____ Date completed _____

Source of data _____ Library _____

Instructions

Purpose of Workform 13

Producing an output frequently involves more than the operational steps in a task. Approval points, storage time, and transporting materials from place to place can add to the time it takes to complete an output. This workform will help you take a larger view of the flow of work through your operations to identify these potential bottlenecks.

Sources of Data for Workform 13

Listing the steps in the task you are studying is the source of data for this workform. The steps you have listed on earlier workforms are those in which staff were actively handling materials (operations steps). In completing Workform 13 you will add, in the correct sequence, steps that involve other types of actions.

Factors to Consider When Completing Workform 13

1. Keep these definitions in mind for the four types of steps as you complete the workform:

   operations—a step of actively handling materials to create an output

   transport—the movement of inputs from one place to another during an activity or task

   approval—a stopping point at which no further activity takes place until approval is given

   storage—setting inputs aside at the end of a step until some other step is completed

2. To build a more comprehensive picture of the flow of work, you may list the steps in multiple tasks on a single Workform 13. If you do choose to list multiple tasks, they should be contiguous tasks. This means that the output of one listed task should be the input for the next task you list on the workform.

To Complete Workform 13

1. **Item A** Identify the location and/or work unit where the tasks or activity listed in the workform take place.

2. **Item B** Write the task or activity you are studying. If you intend to list more than one task on the workform, identify the group of tasks you are studying with an activity name. For example, if you are tracking all of the tasks between receipt of a shipment and shelving a book, you might name the activity "acquiring materials."

3. **Item C** Identify the starting point of the activity or task.

4. **Column D** List—in sequence—all of the steps performed for this task or activity. Use another sheet of paper if necessary, but number all of the steps in sequence. There should be no discontinuities in the steps; the ending point of one step should be the starting point of the next step.

   Standard terms to describe tasks and steps may have been developed by the library as a part of this data-gathering process. If so, use those terms here. Check with the person who asked you to complete this workform to determine if standard terms exist.

   Supplement the standard operations steps with descriptions of the transport, approval, and storage steps in the tasks listed.

   At the end of each row listing a step, mark one of the four boxes to indicate if the listed step is an operation, a transport step, an approval step, or a storage point.

5. **Item E** Identify the end point of the task or activity.

Factors to Consider When Reviewing Workform 13

1. How many approval points appear on the list? Are all of these approvals needed?

2. Are the approval points actually quality-control checks? If so, does the error rate warrant the number of quality checkpoints you see?

3. How many storage steps appear on the list? Do these steps indicate multiple instances of handling materials, i.e., moving materials from book trucks to shelves, then back to book trucks?

4. Is timely output important to the customer? If so, how do the storage steps affect the timeliness of the outputs?

WORKFORM 13 Workflow Chart

A. Location and/or work unit: _____

B. Task or activity: _____

C. Starting point of task or activity: _____

D. Steps in the Task or Activity

	Operation*	Transport*	Approval*	Storage*
1.	○	△	◇	□
2.	○	△	◇	□
3.	○	△	◇	□
4.	○	△	◇	□
5.	○	△	◇	□
6.	○	△	◇	□
7.	○	△	◇	□
8.	○	△	◇	□
9.	○	△	◇	□
10.	○	△	◇	□
11.	○	△	◇	□
12.	○	△	◇	□

E. End point of task or process: _____

*Definitions:
○ *Operation*—a step of actively handling materials to create an output
△ *Transport*—the movement of inputs from one place to another during an activity
◇ *Approval*—a stopping point at which no further activity takes place until approval is given
□ *Storage*—setting inputs aside at the end of a step until some other step is completed

Completed by _____ Date completed _____

Source of data _____ Library _____

Index

A

activities
    defined, 7
    describing, 37, 47, 49
    process analysis of, 10
    relationship to tasks and
        steps, 8, 9
    time spent on, 54, 55, 126–30
    who performs, 48, 120–1
    in workload analysis project,
        37–8
advisory groups, 16–17, 26–7, 28,
    31, 95
approval, 84, 89, 99
assumptions, 23
audiences, 95–8
averages, 79–80

B

baselines
    comparing measures, 57, 59,
        78
    defined, 7
    establishing, 9, 19, 36, 43, 45
brainstorming, 30–1
budget, project, 35

C

central tendency, 80
change, 3–4, 17–18, 95
    approval for, 99
    communicating, 96
    and process analysis, 19–20,
        62
    resistance to, 12, 99–104
charts, 97–8
climate, 12–13, 15
communication, 12, 13–16
    and advisory groups, 16, 28
    of changes, 101

    lack of, 100
    methods of, 15–16, 25
    planning, 95–6
    of project results, 95–9
continuous quality improvement,
    26–7, 62, 78
culture, 12–13, 15, 26
customers, 10, 68
cycles, improvement, 108–9

D

data
    analyzing, 66, 68–76
    collecting, 26–7, 37, 38–40
    and decision making, 6–7
    existing, 43–5
data spreads, 80–1
decisions, 2, 6–7
detail, level of, 37
diagrams, 98
direct observation log, 58, 135–8.
    See also observation

E

effectiveness, 4–5, 7, 18
efficiency, 4–5, 7
effort. *See also* time
    data on, 46–51
    defined, 7–8
    in input-driven tasks, 72
    numeric analysis of, 9
    and output, 52–7
employee associations, 25
employees, involvement of, 25
environment, 59, 84–5

F

facts, 102
feedback, 107

floor plans, 91, 98
flow diagrams, 89, 91, 92
flowcharts, 91–2

G

goals, library, 5, 7, 17, 23
goals, of workload analysis
    project, 38
goals, project
    negotiation of, 102–3
    and project overview, 38,
        112–16
    scope of, 43
    and success indicators, 106–7
    and who does what, 47
graphs, 97–8

H

Hawthorne effect, 57
hot spots, 30–2
hours available, 41, 117–19

I

implementation, 105–8
information needs, 14–16
inputs, defined, 8, 62
intuition, 2, 5–6

L

longitudinal studies, 8, 10, 36, 49

M

macroprocesses versus
    microprocesses, 63–4
maps, 98
mean (arithmetic), 79–80
measures, library, 3–4

median (arithmetic), 79–80
methodology, 102, 103
mind mapping, 30–1
mission, library, 23
mode (arithmetic), 80
morale, 13
multivariate analysis, 83–5

N
narratives, 97
National Center for Education
Statistics (NCES), 39–40
negotiation, 102
numeric analysis
baseline measures, 36, 45, 57,
59
defined, 7, 8–10, 19
effort and output, establishing
link between, 52–7
effort, developing data on,
46–51
and observation, 53, 57
output data, using, 43–5
and performance assessment,
36
and self-reporting, 53
and vocabulary, standard,
47–51
numeric measures
analyzing, 78–86
defined, 8

O
observation, 53, 65–6, 67, 140–1
of demand-driven tasks, 74
direct observation log, 57, 58,
135–8
operation steps, 89
output statistics, 39
outputs
defined, 8, 62
of input-driven tasks, 72
measuring, 43, 44, 45
and numeric analysis, 7, 9, 36,
43
and process analysis, 10, 62
and staff hours worked
(effort), 46
time to produce, 89

P
percentages, 81–2
percentiles, 82–3
performance assessment, 8, 36

performance measurement, 8, 9,
10–11
performance-based evaluation
programs, 78
persuasion, 96–7
pilot projects, 106
planning, 22–8
assumptions, 23
and communication, 28
and data gathering, 27
and project design, 26–7
and project implementation,
28
purpose of project, 23–4
questions to ask, 24–5
precision, 9, 11, 38–40, 47
presentation of project results,
97–8
pretesting, 47, 49
problem solving, 10–11, 17–18,
36, 62–3
process analysis, 10–12
choosing, 62–3
defined, 7, 19
detailed, 86–93
and problem solving, 36–7
process reengineering, 62
productivity, 79
public service desks, 49, 51, 85–6,
88–9, 151–3
purpose of workload analysis,
23–4

Q
quality checkpoints, 84

R
rankings, 85, 86
resistance to change, 12, 99–104
resource allocation, 2
rolling implementation, 106

S
School Improvement Act of 1988
(PL 100-297), 39
self-reporting, 53, 56, 65–6,
132–4, 142–3
SMART acronym, 30
spreadsheets, 97–8
staff
communicating with, 14–15,
95
hours worked and output
produced, 46

involvement of, 25
observing, 58, 135–8
productive hours available, 41,
117–19
self-reporting, 56, 132–4
task analysis, 131–8
time analysis, 54, 55, 126–30
staged implementation, 106
standards, 78
steps
defined, 8
describing, 11, 50, 65–6,
122–5
in input-driven tasks, 72–3
process analysis of, 10, 62,
86–7
relationship to activities and
tasks, 8, 9
in tasks, 37, 65–6, 68–70
time required for, 70–6
types of, 89
value-added versus nonvalue-
added, 68–9, 87
storage points, 84, 89
success, measuring, 106–7

T
tables, 97–8
task analysis
observation, 67, 140–1
self-report, 142–3
tasks
defined, 8, 62
describing, 11, 47, 49, 50,
122–5
demand-driven, 70, 72, 73–6,
148–50
input-driven, 70, 71–3, 145–7
process analysis of, 10, 62
relationship to activities and
steps, 8, 9
sequencing, 35
staff performance of, 131–8
starting and ending points,
64–5
steps in, 37, 65–6, 68–70
variations in, 66, 84
who performs, 48, 120–1
time. *See also* effort
estimates of, 52–3
to produce outputs, 89
spent on demand-driven tasks,
70, 72, 73–6, 148–50
spent on input-driven tasks,
70, 71–3, 145–7
spent on public desks, 151–3

and staffing decisions, 4–6
variables affecting, 84
work hours available, 41,
  117–19
total quality management
  (TQM), 26–7, 59, 62, 108
transport steps, 89
Tree County Public Library, 5–6,
  25–6, 32, 43–4, 51, 57, 72–3,
  87–8, 98–9, 104
trends, 8, 36

U
unions, 12, 25, 95, 99

V
values, 12–13, 15, 102, 103
variances, 78, 83–4
vocabulary, 47–51, 66, 68

W
work distribution, 5–6
workflow, 65, 89–93, 90,
  154–5
workload analysis
  activities in, 37–8
  approaches to, 36–7
  approval for, 35–6
  assumptions, 23

constraints of, 30
defined, 7–12
design of, 26
flowchart, 34
goal of, 29–30, 47
implementation of, 28
management of, 28–36
outline, 32–5
project overview, 112–16
purpose of, 17–18, 23–4,
  36–40
responsibilities, 35
sequence, 35
staff involvement, 25
workloads, 6–7, 9, 78

Diane Mayo is vice president of Information Partners, Inc., an information technology and library automation and management consulting firm that specializes in assisting libraries with planning and implementing a wide range of technologies. She has more than twenty years' experience as a librarian, much of it focused on managing technology. Mayo has managed both technical services and public services in multi-branch public libraries. She is coauthor of *Wired for the Future: Developing Your Library Technology Plan* (ALA, 1999) and of *Managing for Results: Effective Resource Allocation for Public Libraries* (ALA, 2000).

Jeanne Goodrich is a consultant and trainer who specializes in public library planning, job analysis, and data collection and analysis. She was formerly deputy director of the Multnomah County Library in Portland, Oregon. Goodrich has more than thirty years of experience in public library management, including directing medium-sized libraries and serving as deputy director for library development at a state library agency.